Urban Land Acquisition and Involuntary Resettlement

DIRECTIONS IN DEVELOPMENT
Environment and Sustainable Development

Urban Land Acquisition and Involuntary Resettlement

Linking Innovation and Local Benefits

Vincent Roquet, Luciano Bornholdt, Karen Sirker, and Jelena Lukic

WORLD BANK GROUP

Contents

Boxes

Maps

Photos

Table

Foreword

Our planet is undergoing a process of rapid urbanization. Although the past century witnessed a massive increase in built-up urban spaces, it pales in comparison to what lies ahead. More than half of the eventual urban footprint of our planet expected by 2030 is yet to be built. The next few decades will see growth in urban areas, including in urban infrastructure, at a pace and scale that have not been experienced. Ninety percent of the growth in the urban footprint will take place in low- and middle-income countries (LMICs).

The expansion and development of urban areas require the acquisition of land, which often requires physical relocation of people who own or occupy that land. Land acquisition and resettlement may also be required to improve the lives of the more than 1 billion people who live in slums around the world, most of them in LMICs. Therefore, any effort to embark on significant, sustainable urban development must ensure that there are adequate processes for land acquisition so that resettlement does not constrain much-needed urban development.

Going beyond simply ensuring that there are adequate resettlement processes, urban planners, architects, policy makers, and social scientists can afford to be more ambitious. They can try to implement urban development programs in a way that enables the people who lose their land, houses, or livelihoods to become equal partners in the development process and to benefit as much from the programs as the other residents who share the urban space with them. The combination of the high price of urban land, the presence of creative individuals in close proximity in urban areas, and the tendency of urban space to generate innovative solutions can help convert urban resettlement into a development opportunity for all.

The examples discussed in this report illustrate how urban resettlement can become a development opportunity for those who are ostensibly adversely affected by the process of urban development. The Mumbai example shows how the private sector can play a key role in unleashing the potential created by high-value land to provide sustainable housing solutions to those adversely affected at no cost to the government or the resettlers. Examples from Morocco and Pakistan show how well-designed and well-implemented citizen-driven resettlement can result in enhanced skills and livelihoods and can promote overall sustainable urban development. The Mauritania example demonstrates how collective approaches with strong community participation can help address difficult challenges related to housing. Finally, the Brazil case shows how resettlement practices with demonstrated positive outcomes and contributions to urban development can influence governments to incorporate the practices into their own laws and regulations and can benefit the millions of affected people beyond World Bank–supported projects.

I am sure this report will inspire urban development specialists and resettlement professionals to work together to develop approaches that help convert urban resettlement into a development opportunity. I also hope that, at the institutional level, it will prompt the World Bank and other international development organizations to actively work with national and regional governments to support them in strengthening their own policies and institutional frameworks on land acquisition and resettlement. By doing so, we could help spread the benefits of these win-win approaches to urban development to millions of people around the world.

Maninder Gill,
Director, Social Development,
Global Unit, GSURR

Acknowledgments

The preparation of this case study report was coordinated by a team consisting of Vincent Roquet (team leader), Luciano Bornholdt, Karen Sirker, and Jelena Lukic from the Global Unit of the World Bank's Social, Urban, Rural and Resilience (GSURR) Global Practice. The team worked under the guidance of Susan Wong, Practice Manager, Social Development, Global Unit, and Maninder Gill, Director, Social Development, Global Unit, GSURR.

The team benefited from comments provided by the following peer reviewers: Afshan H. Khawaja, Chaohua Zhang, Chaogang Wang, and Jorge E. Villegas of GSURR; Glenn S. Morgan and Peter Leonard of Operations Risk Management; and Sameh Naguib Wahba, Practice Manager, Urban and Disaster Risk Management (DRM), Global Unit, GSURR. The team also benefited from specific comments provided by Alberto Coelho Gomes Costa of GSURR and Marcos Thadeu Abicalil of the Water Global Practice (GWADR) on the Brazil country systems case study; from other comments provided by Edda Mwakselo Ivan Smith, Chisako Fukuda, Kimberley M. Borrows, and Narae Choi of GSURR; as well as from advice kindly provided by Jonathan M. Lindsay of the Environmental and International Law Department (LEGEN) and by Dan Gibson and Gordon Appleby, resettlement consultants.

Moreover, the team wishes to thank the following people for their key contributions to the case study reports:

- **Brazil country systems case study:** Fabio Pittaluga, GSURR; Anaclaudia Rossbach, Latin America and the Caribbean Regional Advisor for the Cities Alliance; Francesco di Villarosa, international consultant; and Sameh Naguib Wahba, Practice Manager, Urban and DRM, Global Unit, GSURR
- **Mumbai, India, Urban Transport Project case study:** Satya N. Mishra and I. U. B. Reddy, GSURR
- **Mauritania Urban Development Project case study:** Brahim Abdelwedoud, GSURR; and Christian Diou, former task team leader
- **Morocco Artisan and Fez Medina Project case study:** Jonathan Richart, Senior Director and Global Practice Lead, Environmental and Social Performance, Millennium Challenge Corporation; Houcine Gabi, Director, Environment,

Agence de Partenariat pour le Progrès; and Said Abouyacoub, Manager, Social Unit, Agence de Dédensification et de Réhabilitation de Fès
- **Sustainable Development of the Walled City Lahore, Pakistan, Project case study:** Shahnaz Arshad and Salma Omar, GSURR.

The team also wishes to thank Sara Proehl and Marcy Gessel for editing the report; Mary Fisk and Jewel McFadden for managing the production process; Naylor Design and Datapage for providing the design and layout; and Colum Garrity, Syed Abdul Salam, Anju Sachdeva, and Cristal Llave for providing timely support to facilitate the completion of the report. Special thanks are extended to the following for photographs and maps included in the report: Satya N. Mishra for the India case study, Brahim Abdelwedoud for the Mauritania case study, Vincent Roquet and the Millennium Challenge Corporation for the Morocco case study, and Shahnaz Arshad for the Pakistan case study.

About the Authors

Vincent Roquet, a Canadian national, has 30 years of private and public sector experience in social development, environmental management, and urban planning. Before joining the World Bank as a Senior Social Development Specialist in 2013, he was the president of his own environmental and social consulting firm in Montreal. He has a master's degree in urban planning from the University of Montreal, Canada.

Luciano Bornholdt, a Brazilian national, has more than 10 years of experience in social studies in low- and middle-income countries, with a particular focus on Latin America. Before joining the World Bank as a Senior Social Development Specialist in 2013, he worked at the Inter-American Development Bank. He has a PhD in social anthropology from the University of Manchester, United Kingdom.

Karen Sirker, an American national, worked for nearly 30 years at the World Bank as a Senior Knowledge and Learning Officer and as a Senior Social Development Specialist, including 12 years at the World Bank Institute. She has an MA in international economics and social change and development from the John Hopkins University, Baltimore, Maryland, United States.

Jelena Lukic, a Serbian national, has nearly 10 years of experience working as a Social Development Specialist for the World Bank Group, including 3 years at the International Finance Corporation. She has a master's degree in international business and conflict resolution from Tufts University, Medford, Massachusetts, United States.

Glossary

The following definitions are largely drawn from the World Bank's *Involuntary Resettlement Sourcebook* (2004a), the International Finance Corporation's *Handbook for Preparing a Resettlement Action Plan* (2002), and the World Bank's "Position Paper on Squatters and Encroachers" (Gill and others 2000).

Affectees, displaced persons, affected persons, or project-affected persons: The people or entities directly affected by a project through the loss of land and the resulting loss of residences, other structures, businesses, or other assets. Such persons can be physically displaced or economically displaced through a loss of income streams or livelihoods resulting from land acquisition or obstructed access to resources (land, water, or forest).

Asset inventory: A complete count and description of all property and assets that will be acquired.

Compensation: Payment in cash or in kind for an asset or a resource that is acquired or affected by a project at the time the asset needs to be replaced.

Cutoff date: Date of completion for the census and assets inventory of project-affected persons. Persons occupying the project area after the cutoff date are not eligible for compensation or resettlement assistance.

Eligibility: The qualification criteria for receiving benefits under a resettlement program. These criteria serve as the basis for defining resettlement entitlements accrued to each eligibility category—such as affected residential or commercial property owners, renters, vendors, and squatters.

Eminent domain: The right of the state to acquire land, using its sovereign power, for public purpose. National law establishes which public agencies have the prerogative to exercise eminent domain.

Grievance procedures or grievance redress mechanisms: The processes established under law, local regulations, or administrative decisions to enable property owners and other displaced persons to redress issues related to acquisition, compensation, and other aspects of resettlement.

Host community (hosts): The population in areas receiving resettlers. Special attention must be paid to the needs and concerns of the host community/hosts in a resettlement program to minimize social risks and avoid potential social conflicts.

Informal urban occupations: Informal or irregular urban occupations are defined as unregistered fixed, transient, or mobile commercial or artisanal activities in urban settings, such as those conducted by street vendors, weekly market vendors, and traditional artisanal producers and vendors. Such vendors and producers are generally characterized by high rates of poverty, income insecurity, and limited official recognition of their rights to practice their occupations in the sites that they occupy.

Informal urban settlements: Informal or irregular urban settlements—or slums—are defined as unplanned and unauthorized urban developments in vacant urban land, such as designated industrial or commercial development zones, airport domains, port facilities, parks, protected areas, hillsides, flood-prone areas, disused estates, or the unused margins of formal rights-of-way. They are generally characterized by rapid and disorderly growth; high rates of poverty and social exclusion; limited access to public infrastructure and services, such as transportation, water, health, and education; and frequent exposure to violence and crime.

Initial baseline survey: The population census, asset inventory, and socioeconomic survey together constitute the baseline survey of an affected population. When properly conducted, an initial baseline survey can be used as a baseline reference for monitoring and evaluation activities.

Land acquisition: The process of acquiring land under the legally mandated procedures of eminent domain.

OP (Operational Policy) 4.12: The World Bank's operational policy on involuntary resettlement that defines borrower requirements applicable to land acquisition, restrictions on land use, and involuntary resettlement. The policy objectives of OP 4.12 are as follows:

- Involuntary resettlement should be avoided, when feasible, or minimized, exploring all viable project designs.
- When it is not feasible to avoid involuntary resettlement, resettlement activities should be conceived and executed as sustainable development programs, providing sufficient investment resources to enable the persons displaced by the project to share in project benefits. Displaced persons should be meaningfully consulted and have opportunities to participate in the planning and implementation of resettlement programs.
- Displaced persons should be assisted in their efforts to improve their livelihoods and standards of living, or to at least restore them, in real terms, to pre-displacement levels or to levels prevailing prior to the beginning of project implementation, whichever is higher.

Population census: A complete and accurate count of the population that is affected by land acquisition and related impacts. When properly conducted, a population census provides the basic information necessary for determining compensation eligibility.

Project cycle: The process of identifying, planning, approving, and implementing a World Bank–supported development activity. A World Bank project cycle is divided into the following stages: identification, preparation, appraisal, negotiations, approval, loan effectiveness, and implementation. If land acquisition, restriction of access to land, or involuntary resettlement is likely to occur, resettlement instruments such as resettlement action plans or resettlement policy frameworks must be prepared by the borrower before appraisal.

Relocatees, relocated communities, or resettlers: Groups of people who have to move to new locations as a result of projects.

Resettlement action plan/resettlement plan (RAP): A resettlement action plan (or resettlement plan) is a planning document describing what will be done to address the direct social and economic impacts associated with project-specific involuntary taking of land or restriction of access to land. Other social and economic impacts not associated with land takings and restrictions are dealt with through a project-specific environmental and social management plan. The required contents of a resettlement action plan are described in annex A of the World Bank's OP 4.12.

Resettlement entitlements: The sum total of compensation and other forms of assistance provided to displaced persons in respective eligibility categories.

Resettlement, livelihood restoration, or economic rehabilitation strategy: The approaches used to assist people in their efforts to improve (or at least restore) their incomes, livelihoods, and standards of living in real terms after resettlement. The resettlement strategy typically consists of payment of compensation at replacement cost, transition support arrangements, relocation to new sites (if applicable), and assistance to help convert income-generating assets into income streams.

Resettlement policy framework: A document describing the resettlement principles, the organizational arrangements, and the design criteria applied to undefined subprojects prepared during project implementation. A resettlement action plan (or resettlement plan) must be prepared for each subproject once its footprint has been properly defined. The corresponding document for other social and economic impacts not associated with land takings and restrictions is an environmental and social management framework. The required contents of a resettlement policy framework are described in annex A of the World Bank's OP 4.12.

Socioeconomic survey: A complete and accurate survey of the project-affected population. Surveys focus on income-earning activities and other socioeconomic indicators.

Squatters or encroachers: Whether classified as squatters or encroachers, occupants of informal urban settlements can be divided into three broad categories, depending on the length of occupancy and the legitimacy of their claims to acquired rights:

1. People with longstanding and sometimes even ancestral claims to the lands they occupy.
2. People who have occupied land more recently, many by reason of requiring residential space in urban areas to which they or their forebears have migrated, and others because they have moved into disused estates or into the unused margins of formal rights-of-way, including "pavement dwellers" and occupants of traffic islands, roadsides, and railway tracks and yards.
3. People who move into announced project areas or other zones, opportunistically seeking to receive benefits under a resettlement or other government program.

There is a consensus that people opportunistically invading project areas after projects are announced (category 3) should not be entitled to resettlement assistance. However, discussions with borrowers typically reflect areas of ambiguity in World Bank policy regarding squatters and encroachers who fall under category 2 and who typically claim use rights or even ownership of public land following some period of uncontested or de facto recognized occupation, utilization, or investment.

Stakeholders: A broad term that covers all parties affected by or interested in a project or a specific issue—in other words, all parties that have a stake in a particular issue or initiative. *Primary stakeholders* are those most directly affected by a project—in resettlement situations, these individuals represent the population that loses property or income because of the project as well as the host communities. Other people who have an interest in the project— such as the project authority itself, the beneficiaries of the project, and interested nongovernmental organizations—are termed *secondary stakeholders*.

Vulnerable groups or persons: OP 4.12 requires that particular attention be paid to the needs of vulnerable groups or persons among those displaced, especially people living below the poverty line, the landless, the elderly, women, children, indigenous peoples, ethnic minorities, and other displaced persons who may not be protected through national land compensation legislation.

Abbreviations

ADER-Fès	Agence de Dédensification et de Réhabilitation de Fès (Morocco)
ADU	Agence de Développement Urbain (Mauritania)
AMEXTIPE	Agence Mauritanienne d'Exécution des Travaux d'Intérêt Public pour l'Emploi (Mauritania)
APL	adaptable program loan (World Bank)
APP	Agence du Partenariat pour le Progrès (Morocco)
CBOs	community-based organizations
CDHLCPI	Commissariat aux Droits de l'Homme, à la Lutte Contre la Pauvreté et à l'Insertion (Mauritania)
DCR	development control regulation
EIA	Estudo de Impacto Ambiental (environmental impact assessment—Brazil)
FSI	floor space index
GIS	geographic information system
GRC	Grievance Redressal Committee (Lahore, Pakistan)
GSURR	Social, Urban, Rural and Resilience Global Practice (World Bank)
GWADR	Water Global Practice
IFC	International Finance Corporation
IPCC	International Panel on Climate Change
JVLR	Jogeshwari Vikhroli Link Road (Mumbai, India)
LAA	Land Acquisition Act of 1894 (Pakistan)
LAC	Latin America and the Caribbean Region (World Bank)
LEGEN	Environmental and International Law Department (World Bank)
LMICs	low- and middle-income countries
MCC	Millennium Challenge Corporation (United States)
MCGM	Municipal Corporation of the Greater Mumbai

MLARR	Management of Land Acquisition, Resettlement and Rehabilitation (Brazil)
MMRDA	Mumbai Metropolitan Region Development Authority
MSRDC	Maharashtra State Road Development Corporation (Mumbai)
MUTP	Mumbai Urban Transport Project
MUTP-2A	Mumbai Urban Transport Project—Phase 2A
NGOs	nongovernmental organizations
OPSOR	Operations Risk Management Department (World Bank)
PAC	Growth Acceleration Program (Programa de Aceleração do Crescimento—Brazil)
PAC2	Second Growth Acceleration Program (Programa de Aceleração do Crescimento—Brazil)
PAP	project-affected person
PLY	Place Lalla Ydouna (Fez, Morocco)
RAP	resettlement action plan/resettlement plan
RAS	reimbursable advisory services (World Bank)
R&R	resettlement and rehabilitation
SAGs	social activist groups (Lahore, Pakistan)
SCLR	Santa Cruz–Chembur Link Road (Mumbai)
SDU	social development unit (Mumbai)
SDWCLP	Sustainable Development of Walled City Lahore Project
SMT	social mobilization team (Lahore, Pakistan)
TDR	transfer of development rights
TISS	Tata Institute of Social Sciences (India)
TMA	Tehsil Municipal Administration (Punjab, Pakistan)
UDP	Urban Development Project (Mauritania)
UGP	Unité de Gestion de Projet (Project Management Unit–Fez, Morocco)
UNESCO	United Nations Educational, Scientific and Cultural Organization
WCL	Walled City of Lahore
WCLA	Walled City of Lahore Authority

Overview

Context

With rapid urbanization and an increasing number of publicly funded urban projects, there is a growing demand to address complex land acquisition and involuntary resettlement issues in urban settings. Major urban projects in such areas as urban development, renewal or upgrading, urban transport, urban watershed management, water supply and sanitation, and urban solid waste management require substantial land acquisition and resettlement efforts that raise significant risks to people and investments. Governments and international financing institutions must identify these risks early and manage them adequately.

Complex challenges involved in urban land acquisition and involuntary resettlement include the following:

- Rapidly increasing property values and limited availability of land in downtown areas
- Extended informal settlements in strategic or vulnerable urban areas
- Limited recognition of the rights of residential and commercial renters or de facto occupants of urban spaces
- Urban crime and violence
- Severe transportation bottlenecks
- Complex solid waste management problems
- Critical water and wastewater management issues
- Socioeconomically marginalized urban populations.

These issues are amplified by global trends, such as the degradation of the natural resource base and climate change.

The selection of case studies in this report came about as a result of discussions within the community of World Bank involuntary resettlement practitioners, who agreed that urban resettlement issues remain relatively unexplored and that the greatest need for examples of innovative practices in resettlement was in urban settings. Particularly difficult topics identified in urban resettlement were the following:

- How to bring about improved country systems for urban land acquisition and involuntary resettlement through policy changes
- How to address challenges related to the relocation of large-scale informal urban settlements or slums
- How to address challenges related to livelihood restoration for informal urban occupations.

Scope and Methodology

This report offers case study examples of innovative and successful practices in urban resettlement with the aim of making those examples available for World Bank task teams and client countries. The report was prepared using interviews and desk reviews of selected World Bank Group projects and relevant projects supported by other international financing institutions and donor agencies employing the World Bank's Operational Policy on Involuntary Resettlement (OP 4.12), such as the Millennium Challenge Corporation.

The five selected case studies cover four of the five World Bank regions: Latin America and the Caribbean, Middle East and North Africa, South Asia, and Sub-Saharan Africa. The case studies include, by theme, the following:

- *Improved country systems for urban land acquisition and involuntary resettlement through policy change:* World Bank—Ordinance 317 on Resettlement of the Ministry of Cities of Brazil.
- *Challenges related to the relocation of informal urban settlements:* World Bank—Mumbai Urban Transport Project, India; and World Bank—Urban Development Project in Nouakchott, Mauritania.
- *Challenges related to livelihood restoration for informal urban occupations:* Millennium Challenge Corporation—Artisan and Fez Medina Project, Morocco; and World Bank—Sustainable Development of Walled City Lahore Project, Pakistan.

Innovative Country Systems: Brazil

World Bank—Ordinance 317 on Resettlement of the Ministry of Cities of Brazil

This case study looks at the cooperative process established between the World Bank and the Brazilian Ministry of Cities that led to the issuance of Ordinance 317 by the ministry. The ordinance became official in July 2013 after a two-year process of public consultation and debate among critical stakeholders, such as local governments, private sector companies, and representatives of civil society. The ordinance directly applies to projects and programs funded by the Ministry of Cities, which is in charge of most urban investments under the second

Brazilian Growth Acceleration Program (PAC2). Many of the previously existing gaps between the World Bank's resettlement policy and Brazilian resettlement practices and regulations were bridged through the publication of the ordinance.

The World Bank is now preparing a reimbursable advisory services project to help the Ministry of Cities build capacity in Brazilian municipalities for changing resettlement practices according to the new ordinance. Capacity-building initiatives are expected to result in a large number of public servants who will become versed in resettlement practices informed by international best practices. This is likely to have an impact on tens of billions of U.S. dollars of municipal investments in Brazil over the coming years. The changes in resettlement practices triggered by this process coupled with an increase in capacity in municipalities are also likely to influence other ongoing resettlement practices in the country.

Relocation of Informal Urban Settlements: India and Mauritania

World Bank—Mumbai Urban Transport Project, India
The Mumbai Urban Transport Project (MUTP) involved a resettlement program for about 100,000 informal occupants of slums along a railway line in Mumbai. Although this major resettlement program, implemented with World Bank assistance, was successful and innovative, certain resettlement issues led to project funding being withheld until problems were corrected. Overall, the MUTP presents a good practice case study for urban resettlement because it introduced innovative approaches that were subsequently applied to other urban projects in India. Good practices documented in the case study include the following:

- The application of market-based solutions, such as transfer of development rights as a tradable benefit in lieu of land compensation for resettlement operations in urban slums, which enabled public authorities to encourage private sector developers to fund the resettlement of slum dwellers from horizontally spread-out slums with few community services to modern, multistory buildings in fully serviced resettlement colonies
- The use of self-administered socioeconomic baseline surveys for resettlement of urban slums, with the assistance of local nongovernmental organizations
- The successful capacity building of Mumbai's municipal resettlement authority.

World Bank—Urban Development Project in Nouakchott, Mauritania
An urban resettlement program conducted for the Urban Development Project (UDP) in the largest slum of Nouakchott—the El Mina *kebbe*—was successfully completed in 2004 with the relocation of 2,300 households to a properly serviced urban area located less than a kilometer away. The integrated urban planning and participatory approach adopted for this resettlement operation was selected as an example of good practice for a number of reasons: its successful outcomes were confirmed by independent monitoring and evaluation, it was widely disseminated on the basis of an urban resettlement guidance document,

and it was eventually replicated in other slums in the capital and in other cities by the government of Mauritania with local funding. Good practices documented in the case study include the following:

- Large-scale socioeconomic household surveys conducted by UDP before and after the resettlement program to evaluate the extent to which resettlement outcomes in the El Mina *kebbe* were successful and livelihoods were restored after project completion
- The culturally and socially adapted on-site, state-subsidized, collective housing credit scheme called "Twize" that was developed in response to UDP's objective of reducing poverty through access to decent housing. This approach was based on collective community participation combined with community and solidarity programs to finance and build housing "modules" (a room or plot enclosure and a latrine) for poor families.

Livelihood Restoration for Informal Urban Occupations: Morocco and Pakistan

Millennium Challenge Corporation—Artisan and Fez Medina Project, Morocco

Resettlement for this recently completed project was carried out according to the World Bank's involuntary resettlement policy. It involved relocating an informal sector artisanal production chain from the historic Fez Medina to a small industrial park on the outskirts of the medina. Of particular interest are (a) the approach adopted by the U.S. and Moroccan governments in which resettlement responsibilities were shared according to the respective levels of expertise required and (b) the participatory livelihood restoration approaches developed to maintain the integrity of the production chain during the resettlement process.

Elements of the resettlement plan that proved to be highly successful include the following:

- Financial assistance for specially tailored functional literacy programs and technical training programs provided through an artisanal training center and other registered training centers for female project-affected person (PAP) employees and underage PAP apprentices (ages 15–18), with a 100 percent participation rate
- Financial assistance for the return to school of PAP employees ages 15 or younger. Vocational training programs and functional literacy programs enabled a number of female employees to opt for new career paths.

World Bank—Sustainable Development of Walled City Lahore Project, Pakistan

Resettlement for this recently completed project in the ancient Walled City of Lahore was selected as a case study because of the special care that was taken to assist informal sector shopkeepers and employees, households, and residents in sustaining their livelihoods. It featured a highly successful model of social mobilization for buy-in and engagement from PAPs; benefit-sharing through a livelihoods lens; citizen-led regeneration; and a consistent and field-based monitoring and oversight strategy. The combination of stakeholder engagement and adaptive management led to agreement on contentious issues, to innovative solutions, and to the implementation of an effective resettlement plan.

Conclusions and Recommendations

Although the challenges of each urban resettlement operation are unique, commonalities can be seen among successful approaches, some of which have been promoted by resettlement specialists for a long time. These success factors are summarized as follows:

- *Transparency and participation.* Sometimes seen by resettlement implementers as weakening their negotiating positions, transparency and participation actually increase the likelihood of a successful outcome. The Mumbai case study is remarkable for its use of participatory slum enumeration and resettlement planning with the assistance of local nongovernmental organizations. The Lahore case study featured a highly successful model of social mobilization for achieving buy-in and engagement from PAPs.

- *Understanding of informal economic and social networks.* All four of the project-specific case studies in the report highlight the need to properly understand informal economic and social networks that are affected by resettlement and to define the areas of influence and the impacts of resettlement operations. Gaining this understanding is largely done through participatory studies carried out in informal residential and commercial communities, including through systematic analysis of informal urban livelihoods—as illustrated in the Fez and Lahore case studies—or through self-administered surveys of local nongovernmental organizations—as illustrated in the Mumbai case study.

- *Adaptive management of resettlement operations.* Backed by contingency budgeting and integrated activity scheduling, adaptive management of resettlement operations can help address unforeseen challenges related to the high levels of complexity in urban areas and their related economic and social networks. Additional supervision resources utilized during resettlement implementation are of equal importance. The need for thorough planning is central, but with this level of complexity, resettlement plans cannot be expected to anticipate all potential outcomes. Successful urban resettlement projects are usually supported by flexible and adaptive planning and implementation processes and by appropriate financial resources.

- *Post-resettlement socioeconomic surveys and independent monitoring and evaluation.* Although resettlement monitoring activities were conducted regularly throughout resettlement implementation for all four of the project-specific case studies covered in the report, only one of the case studies—the Mauritania Urban Development Project—conducted large-scale socioeconomic surveys to evaluate the extent to which resettlement outcomes were successful and livelihoods were restored after the project. The surveys were complemented by independent monitoring and evaluation. Such good practices should be encouraged and budgeted for in complex urban resettlement operations.

• *Local capacity building and dissemination of good urban resettlement practices.* The case studies highlighted the importance of local capacity building in ensuring successful outcomes in urban resettlement. Training, public awareness, and specialized technical assistance funded through the Artisan and Fez Medina Project enabled municipal agencies and concerned populations to gain a better understanding of the resettlement processes conducted according to international standards and to compare the results obtained with previously unsuccessful resettlement efforts conducted in compliance with national standards. In Lahore, Pakistan, institutional capacity to implement the resettlement action plan was strengthened through the training of local authorities and community associations in impact assessment and mitigation, grievance redress mechanisms, public participation, and social mobilization. The development of specialized resettlement sourcebooks for informal urban settlements in Mumbai and Nouakchott also contributed to the dissemination of best practices in other Indian and Mauritanian cities.

• *Integration of the planning of urban resettlement into a wider municipal urban planning and housing policy context.* As illustrated by the Mumbai and Nouakchott case studies, the success of urban resettlement programs is largely related to their successful integration into the wider contexts of urban development and renewal. This successful integration was illustrated in the Mumbai case study when the state government of Maharashtra encouraged private sector participation in the resettlement program by offering additional development rights or transfer of development rights or floor space index to private developers willing to resettle slum dwellers in modern buildings at the developers' own expense. This successful integration was also illustrated in the Nouakchott case study, which was particularly noteworthy for its development of an integrated urban planning approach that allowed resettlement operations conducted for displaced households in the El Mina slum to dovetail with urban renewal operations for the majority of households remaining in the slum.

• *Strengthening of country systems.* Whereas most countries have well-enshrined eminent domain and expropriation laws and procedures, only a very limited number have legal frameworks and procedures ensuring that land acquisition and involuntary resettlement go beyond compensation for lost assets and requiring that affected livelihoods be restored or even improved. The strengthening of country systems aims to address such gaps. The application of international resettlement standards continues to be of central importance in development projects. However, initiatives to strengthen country systems for urban resettlement and urban planning are also needed to allow for a more systemic, national-level approach to build capacity and integrate involuntary resettlement and land acquisition into the larger context of urban development and housing policies and programs.

Clearly, there is a need to further establish links between urban planning and housing policies on the one hand and urban involuntary resettlement practices on the other. Linking these policies and practices could involve, for example, promoting innovative in situ approaches to urban resettlement or combining curative measures (such as slum upgrading to address substandard housing stocks and the lack of tenure security, public infrastructure, and services, as well as related urban involuntary resettlement requirements) with preventive measures (such as affordable land and housing development through formal channels) to address the flow of new housing demands. This report does not touch on important issues relating to the functioning of urban land markets and housing market dynamics in cities and historic centers, and those issues' links to urban involuntary resettlement. It is recommended that a dedicated urban/social working group be set up by the World Bank to further explore these issues.

CHAPTER 1

Introduction

Emerging Trends in Urban Resettlement

The past 50 years have seen an unprecedented growth of cities around the world. It is estimated that another "2.7 billion more people will move into cities by 2030, mostly in developing countries, particularly in Africa and Asia" (Joshi-Ghani 2013). At the current pace and magnitude of urbanization, the built-up area will triple in the next 30 years (Glaeser and Joshi-Ghani 2013, 12). With rapid urbanization and an increasing number of urban projects financed by governments, the World Bank, and other international financial institutions across all regions, there is a growing demand to address complex land acquisition and involuntary resettlement issues in urban settings. Major projects in areas such as urban development, urban renewal or upgrading, urban transport, urban watershed management, urban water supply and sanitation, and urban solid waste management require substantial land acquisition and resettlement efforts. Such efforts raise significant risks to people and investments. Governments and international financing institutions must identify these risks early and manage them adequately.

Complex challenges often arise in urban land acquisition and involuntary resettlement. They include rapidly increasing property values and limited availability of land in downtown areas, extended informal settlements in strategic or vulnerable urban areas, limited recognition of the rights of residential and commercial renters or de facto occupants of urban spaces, urban crime and violence, severe transportation bottlenecks, complex solid waste management problems, critical water and wastewater management issues, and socioeconomically marginalized urban populations.[1] These issues are amplified by global trends linked to the degradation of the natural resource base and to climate change.[2]

The complexity of urban resettlement programs is compounded when it involves large numbers of residents of informal or squatter settlements whose rights to occupy the land are not legally recognized. The complexity is also increased when urban resettlement involves the loss of informal livelihoods that are largely dependent on physical location:

> Affected people have often developed sophisticated livelihood strategies, often based on informal activities that are location dependent just as much as rural livelihoods can be land dependent, and as a result, these livelihoods can be disrupted by physical displacement just as much as farming based households are. This particularly applies to the poorest in the community, whose livelihoods could for example be dependent on hawking near a particular place (a railway station, a bus stop) or recycling refuse from a particular dump. Such income streams are in fact very vulnerable to displacement. (World Bank and Government of Maharashtra 2009)

There is also a growing recognition that urban resettlement is a development challenge that can contribute to the emergence of sustainable and socially inclusive cities. In many countries, urban involuntary resettlement processes are scrutinized under the lens of a legacy in which poor families have been removed from high value areas and sent to peripheral and underserved areas far from their sources of income and social networks. New approaches to urban resettlement that are needed in terms of policies, partnerships, and applicable methods include the following:

- Innovative housing policies adopted by the Ministry of Cities in Brazil
- Public–private sector partnerships and the construction of high rises in downtown cores for the relocation of large squatter settlements in India
- Development of integrated approaches to slum upgrading and relocation of squatter settlements in Mauritania
- Innovative participatory approaches to in situ urban resettlement in Bhutan
- Use of rental grants to remove people from camps and help reduce housing deficits in Haiti
- Development of new production and marketing centers for artisans displaced from a historical medina in Morocco
- Integration of urban planning, land use, housing, and urban participatory processes into resettlement planning in Vietnam.

Need for Urban Resettlement Guidance Materials

Involuntary resettlement has traditionally been considered a rural issue rather than an urban one. The development of resettlement policies and methodologies in the 1980s and 1990s derived from efforts to manage large-scale resettlement and livelihood impacts related to big hydropower projects in Africa, Asia, and Latin America. Controversies associated with such projects attracted the attention of academic researchers and international nongovernmental organizations. A widely held perception was that while rural resettlement was relatively complex because of the dependency of displaced populations on local land assets and the absence of rural markets for the replacement of lost lands, urban resettlement was relatively simpler because of the wider availability of property markets.

For small-scale operations, displaced urban residents could be compensated in cash for the loss of assets. For large-scale operations, urban resettlement was frequently viewed as a reconstruction issue, in which displaced urban residents were removed from urban cores to city fringes and provided with modern housing. Livelihood restoration in urban settings was not seen as a significant issue.

Rural development and related resettlement activities have been extensively covered in research literature and development policies, but urban resettlement issues remain relatively unexplored. The case studies in this report offer examples of innovative and successful practices and analytical approaches for task teams and client countries dealing with large-scale urban land acquisition and involuntary resettlement activities in each of the World Bank's regions. The report aims to complement previous related efforts, such as the 2011 publications *Populations at Risks of Disaster: A Resettlement Guide* and *Preventive Resettlement of Populations at Risk of Disaster: Experiences from Latin America*, as well as the World Bank's *Involuntary Resettlement Sourcebook* (2004) and the International Finance Corporation's *Handbook for Preparing a Resettlement Action Plan* (IFC 2002).

Scope and Methodology

The selection of case studies was based on the following main issues that emerged out of ongoing discussions within the community of World Bank Group resettlement practitioners:

- Improved country systems for urban land acquisition and involuntary resettlement through policy change
- Challenges related to the relocation of informal urban settlements
- Challenges related to livelihood restoration for informal urban occupations.

The identification of potential cases corresponding to these issues was mainly based on suggestions provided by World Bank Community of Practice members. Selected case studies had to be relatively recent and closed. A list of potential case studies was established and available project materials for each were reviewed. Only five case studies were selected to allow for sufficient in-depth analysis of each case. An effort was made to geographically distribute the selection of case studies among the various World Bank regions to the greatest possible extent. The five selected case studies cover four of the World Bank's regions: Africa, Latin America and the Caribbean, Middle East and North Africa, and South Asia.

The report was prepared using interviews and desk reviews of selected World Bank Group projects and relevant projects conducted by other international financing institutions and donor agencies employing the World Bank's Operational Policy on Involuntary Resettlement (OP 4.12) or other similar policies, such as the Millennium Challenge Corporation. Desk reviews were based on project appraisal, supervision, and completion documents as well as on information notes produced by task teams. For the case studies located in Brazil and Fez, Morocco, the reviews were based on the direct resettlement planning and implementation supervision experience of the study members.

Desk reviews were complemented as needed by interviews with task team leaders and social development specialists as well as with relevant stakeholders from outside the World Bank Group or at the Millennium Challenge Corporation. The proposed selection of case studies was circulated to other resettlement practitioners at the World Bank for comments. Subsequent drafts of the case study reports were also circulated to appropriate task team leaders and social development specialists for comments. The case study report was finalized on the basis of inputs provided through this consultation process.

Relevant crosscutting themes addressed in the review of each of the selected case studies included the following:

- Management of social risks
- Gender aspects
- Vulnerable groups
- Consultation and participation
- Land tenure and security
- Grievance mechanisms
- Local capacity building
- Urban poverty.

Selection of Case Studies

The five selected case studies by three theme areas are as follows:

1. Improved country systems for urban land acquisition and involuntary resettlement through policy change
   - *World Bank—Ordinance 317 on Resettlement of the Ministry of Cities of Brazil.* This ordinance represents an interesting policy approach to urban resettlement issues. The World Bank has worked closely with the Brazilian Ministry of Cities on several projects. This case study examines the cooperative process in the issuance of Ordinance 317 by the ministry in 2013. The ordinance bridged many of the previously existing gaps between OP 4.12 and Brazilian resettlement practices and regulations. The World Bank is preparing a reimbursable advisory services project to help the Ministry of Cities build capacity in Brazilian municipalities to change resettlement practices according to the new law. This project will likely prove to be a successful example of country systems development.

2. Challenges related to the relocation of informal urban settlements
   - *World Bank—Mumbai Urban Transport Project, India.* This major project involved large-scale resettlement of informal occupants along a railway line in Mumbai. The resettlement program, implemented with World Bank

assistance, was successful and innovative, even though certain resettlement issues led to project funding being withheld until problems were corrected. Good practices documented in the case study include the use of self-administered socioeconomic baseline surveys for resettlement (with the assistance of local nongovernmental organizations) and successful capacity building of a municipal resettlement authority in Mumbai. Implementation of corrective measures for resettlement related to this project was completed in August 2013.

- *World Bank—Urban Development Project in Nouakchott, Mauritania.* An urban resettlement program conducted for the World Bank–funded Urban Development Project in the largest slum of Nouakchott—the El Mina *kebbe*—was successfully completed in 2004 with the relocation of 2,300 households to a properly serviced urban area located less than a kilometer away. The integrated urban planning and participatory approach adopted for this resettlement operation was selected as a good practice example because (a) it was subjected to independent monitoring and evaluation, (b) it was widely disseminated on the basis of an urban resettlement guidance document, and (c) it was eventually replicated by the government of Mauritania in other slums of the capital and other cities with local funding.

3. Challenges related to livelihood restoration for informal urban occupations
   - *Millennium Challenge Corporation—Artisan and Fez Medina Project, Morocco.* Resettlement for this recently completed project was carried out according to OP 4.12 and involved resettling an informal sector artisanal production chain from the medina to a small industrial park outside the medina. Of particular interest are (a) the approach adopted by the U.S. and Moroccan governments in which resettlement responsibilities were shared according to their respective levels of expertise and (b) the participatory livelihood restoration approaches developed to maintain the integrity of the production chain during the resettlement process.
   - *World Bank—Sustainable Development of Walled City Lahore Project, Pakistan.* Resettlement for this recently completed project was selected as an example of good practice because of the special care taken to assist the informal sector shopkeepers, employees, households, and residents in sustaining their livelihoods using (a) a highly successful model of social mobilization, (b) benefit sharing through a livelihoods lens, (c) citizen-led regeneration, and (d) a consistent and field-based monitoring and oversight strategy.

Contents of Report

The contents of the report are as follows:

- Chapter 2, "Innovative Country Systems"—an example of policy reform in Brazil
- Chapter 3, "Relocation of Informal Urban Settlements"—examples from India and Mauritania

- Chapter 4, "Livelihood Restoration for Informal Urban Occupations"—examples from Morocco and Pakistan
- Chapter 5, "Conclusions"—overview of lessons learned for each case study theme.

Notes

1. Examples of projects in which such issues stand out include urban renewal and water management projects in Hanoi, Jakarta, and Manila in East Asia and Pacific; relocation of squatter settlements in Mumbai in South Asia; mass transportation projects in Brazil in Latin America and the Caribbean; and a toll road and solid waste management project in Dakar in Africa.

2. According to the latest Intergovernmental Panel on Climate Change reports, rising sea levels and more frequent extreme weather events are likely to affect coastal urban areas around the world. "Nearly two-thirds of cities with more than 5 million people are located in low-elevation coastal zones, which contain 13 percent of the world's population" (Glaeser and Joshi-Ghani 2013, 10; drawn from McGranahan, Balk, and Anderson 2007).

References

Glaeser, Edward, and Abha Joshi-Ghani. 2013. "Rethinking Cities: Towards Shared Prosperity." Economic Premise note series, No. 126, October 2013, PREM Network, World Bank, Washington, DC.

IFC (International Finance Corporation). 2002. *IFC Handbook for Preparing a Resettlement Plan.* Washington, DC: IFC.

Joshi-Ghani, Abha. 2013. "Rethinking Cities." *People, Spaces, Deliberation* (blog), World Bank, October 28. http://blogs.worldbank.org/publicsphere.

McGranahan, Gordon, Deborah Balk, and Bridget Anderson. 2007. "The Rising Tide: Assessing the Risks of Climate Change and Human Settlements in Low Elevations Coastal Zones." *Environment and Urbanization* 19 (1): 17–37.

World Bank. 2004. *Involuntary Resettlement Sourcebook: Planning and Implementation in Development Projects.* Washington, DC: World Bank.

———. 2011a. *Populations at Risks of Disaster: A Resettlement Guide,* edited by Elena Correa, with Fernando Ramirez and Haris Sanahuja. Washington, DC: World Bank and GFDRR.

———. 2011b. *Preventive Resettlement of Populations at Risk of Disaster: Experiences from Latin America,* edited by Elena Correa. World Bank and GFDRR, Washington, DC.

World Bank and Government of Maharashtra. 2009. *India—Mumbai Urban Transport Project: Guidance Note on Urban Resettlement.* Washington, DC: World Bank.

CHAPTER 2

Innovative Country Systems: Example from Brazil

Rationale for Case Study Selection

A new involuntary resettlement regulation issued in 2013 by the Ministry of Cities in Brazil has garnered significant interest in the development community. Use of country systems, including institutional practices and applicable laws and regulations, has become increasingly important for environmental and social risk management. Such systems are usually national; subnational (for example, state or municipal); or sectoral (for example, electricity). Brazil's Ordinance (*Portaria*) 317 (Government of Brazil 2013) provides an interesting illustration of some of the ways in which the World Bank can collaborate with borrower countries in the improvement of country systems.

Successful involuntary resettlement has two common elements: detailed planning and an approach that goes beyond simple compliance using certain criteria, including those defined by the World Bank's Operational Policy on Involuntary Resettlement (OP 4.12). For involuntary resettlement to be successful, the focus must be on problem solving. Safeguard policies and improvement of country systems are two approaches to problem solving in resettlement practices. Multilateral development banks, financial institutions, and development agencies are moving toward more intensive and extensive use of country systems for risk management, following the definition of the Millennium Development Goals in 2000, the Monterrey Consensus of 2002, and the Aid Effectiveness Declarations of 2005, 2008, and 2011.

Although countries generally have well-enshrined eminent domain and expropriation laws and procedures, only a few have legal frameworks and procedures aimed at ensuring that land acquisition and involuntary resettlement go beyond compensating for lost assets and require that affected livelihoods be restored or even improved.

Illustrating the tendency toward improvement of country systems, and in similar fashion to Brazil, India passed the Right to Fair Compensation and Transparency in Land Acquisition, Rehabilitation, and Resettlement Act in 2013. This law replaces the Land Acquisition Act of 1894, inherited from the period of

British rule. It covers land acquisition by the central government or by any of the state governments, with the exclusion of Jammu and Kashmir. It also covers the acquisition of lands by the state for the use of private companies for declared public purposes. As in the case of the Brazilian ordinance, this new law better aligns national regulations with applicable international standards. Nevertheless, as in Brazil, one of the challenges lies in its implementation at the national, subnational, and local administrative levels. Between 2006 and 2012, the World Bank provided nonlending technical assistance, which influenced the content of the bill passed in 2013. Although better alignment between World Bank resettlement policy and national regulations simplifies the process of agreeing on approaches for resettlement in World Bank–funded projects, actual policy implementation—and especially institutional capacity for implementation—remains a challenge.

On a broad level, the gap between the World Bank's resettlement policy and current country systems generally remains significant. How to bridge that gap is the subject of extensive international debates among environmental and social safeguard practitioners.

This case study focuses on the development of an innovative policy-level approach to resettlement issues. It illustrates with an existing case the development of country systems in relation to the current safeguard policy approach used by the World Bank in avoiding, mitigating, and compensating resettlement impacts of development interventions. Successful outcomes highlighted in the case study were facilitated by the close relationship developed between the World Bank and the Brazilian Ministry of Cities, as well as collaboration with several municipalities through planning and implementing many complex urban projects over a number of years.

The case study looks specifically at Ordinance 317, which the Ministry of Cities issued in 2013 to bridge many of the gaps previously existing between OP 4.12 and Brazilian involuntary resettlement practices and regulations in urban contexts (Government of Brazil 2013). The case study presents some of the key characteristics of this new legislation as well as some fundamental elements of the context that made its issuing possible.

This ordinance will likely prove to be a successful case of country systems development that both increases compliance with safeguard policies and standards and aligns them with international best practices. As part of the process of cooperation between the World Bank and the Ministry of Cities, the Latin America and the Caribbean (LAC) region of the World Bank is preparing a project in the form of reimbursable advisory services (RAS) to help the ministry build capacity in about 5,000 Brazilian municipalities for the improvement of current resettlement practices in accordance with the new ordinance.

Background

The Ministry of Cities' Ordinance 317 became official in July 2013 after a two-year process of public consultation and debates among critical stakeholders, including local governments, private sector companies, and the Council of

Cities—an urban policy body with representatives from civil society and the public and the private sectors (Government of Brazil 2013).

During discussions to design the regulation, a working group composed of key ministries—human rights, environment, energy, cities, and the president's cabinet—was formed to investigate how families in the main metropolitan areas of Brazil were affected by public works. This investigation reinforced the need for a strong regulatory instrument at the national level and the need for better planning, participation, and sustainable housing developments.

The strong relationship developed between the World Bank's Social and Urban Sector for Brazil and the Ministry of Cities—especially its secretary of housing—allowed for the development of a series of initiatives. One of the initial milestones in the process that led to the passage of Ordinance 317 was the publication of the 2011 World Bank report, "Involuntary Resettlement in Brazil: A Review of Policies and Practices" by the Social Development Unit of the World Bank's LAC region. The report included suggestions for improving involuntary resettlement practices in the country, laying the foundation for a dialogue geared toward preparing a new regulation for involuntary resettlement in the context of the preparations for two major events taking place in Brazil: the 2014 World Cup and the 2016 Olympic Games.

In 2011, the same year the report was published, nonlending technical assistance funded by the Cities Alliance initiative through the Brazil Country Management Unit was put into place. One of the landmarks in the development of the ordinance was the International Workshop on Involuntary Displacement in Brazil, March 27–28, 2012, which was organized by the World Bank and the Brazilian Ministry of Cities with funds from the nonlending technical assistance (World Bank 2012).

The stated objective of the workshop was to find solutions for the infrastructure challenges faced by the country, which were expected to intensify because of the preparations for the World Cup and the Olympic games. To that end, the workshop included specialists and case presentations to support the development of content for an involuntary resettlement ordinance. The workshop was an important step in strengthening the collaboration between the World Bank and the Brazilian government on issues related to resettlement, which already had a strong base through the World Bank's operational work in the country.

The workshop was followed by the World Bank's provision of technical support to the Ministry of Cities in drafting a regulation for involuntary resettlement for projects funded through the ministry's budget. By hiring consultants with a history of working for the ministry and by engaging them along with World Bank specialists, participants were able to leverage existing relationships— both professional and personal. The nonlending technical assistance was also used to fund the participation of a ministry official in a Management of Land Acquisition, Resettlement, and Rehabilitation (MLARR) training course supported by the World Bank's LAC region and conducted by an alliance of Latin American universities in Colombia. Participation in the course helped generate interest and access to technical information that proved to be a key factor in the development of the ordinance.

The wider political context in Brazil and the historical scenario also proved significant. Resettlement processes in Brazilian cities are closely connected to urban development that is largely perceived as part of the country's social legacy. Public pressure has been largely connected to an ongoing gentrification process in large cities and to the presence of civil society organizations active in the housing sector coupled with a view of housing as a basic human right.

During the first half of 2013, broad popular demonstrations took place in Brazil, initially opposing raises in public transportation costs but later against what were perceived as several social needs not being adequately met by the government. The demand for increased dialogue between the government of Brazil and social movements led to a set of measures, including the leveraging of investments in urban mobility, among many others. In this context, the ordinance on involuntary resettlement for urban public works, which was funded by the Ministry of Cities and already in an advanced stage of preparation, was approved and published.

The developments in resettlement regulations in Brazil cannot be credited to a single action or factor. The issuance of the new ordinance came about because of a combination of context, interinstitutional cooperation, and political timing and will.

In many respects, the ordinance resembles the World Bank's Involuntary Resettlement Policy. Nevertheless, the World Bank did not impose its policy requirements on the Ministry of Cities. Rather, the World Bank engaged the ministry in a dialogue on its own terms with the objective that the ministry would resolve its own issues. The fact that the resulting ordinance resembles OP 4.12 could indicate a convergence toward best practices. The World Bank engaged the ministry through dialogue on a specific topic—resettlement—using the approach that a challenge was to be solved rather than taking a technocratic perspective. The participation of civil society in this dialogue was also made possible because the World Bank did not try to push its own agenda of adapting country systems to its own safeguard policies.

Given the nature of this engagement, it took time to get buy-in from a number of stakeholders. The World Bank had to stay the course with developing the dialogue and accepting that local political processes are what ultimately determine whether change will be viable.

Thematic Analysis

Urban Resettlement in Brazil before the Ordinance

Before the publication of the ordinance, Brazil did not have specific national legislation on involuntary resettlement. Landowners affected by development projects were compensated through the application of expropriation legislation. In some cases, because of certain interpretations of the existing law, good-faith squatters were compensated for improvements to the land. The calculation of the compensation, however, took into account the depreciation of such improvements over time.

Beyond expropriation, any other socioeconomic effects of development projects, including those related to land acquisition, were addressed on a case-by-case basis through the environmental licensing process. Urban projects are commonly licensed at the municipality or state level. Specific requirements relating to resettlement were left to the discretion and judgment of technical staff.

The environmental licensing agencies require that the environmental impact assessment (*Estudo de Impacto Ambiental* or EIA) include measures to address social impacts, including those caused by land acquisition. Normally, expropriation issues reflected in the environmental license are restricted to ensuring governmental consent and the issuance of the relevant expropriation decree.

Without an overarching regulatory framework, there were large variations among projects. Landowners were frequently compensated for a loss of assets but not for other costs relating to physical or economic displacement. Furthermore, because the concept of "affected populations" was not determined by regulations, it could vary from project to project and could, therefore, influence the application of entitlements. At times, only property owners were included as affected persons, excluding many other affected people from being entitled to compensation. In other cases, eligibility categories were applied too broadly, creating a financial burden on project implementation and feasibility. Similarly, informal dwellers could either be assisted or excluded in any given resettlement project. Even when nonlandowners were included as beneficiaries of a resettlement plan, procedures defined in the legal and regulatory framework were often limited to compensation for the loss of assets.

Ordinance 317

Since the ordinance's publication in July 2013, some issues common to resettlement have been regulated, at least in the portfolio of the Ministry of Cities. The ordinance itself begins with a reference to international treaties and national laws—among them the Federal Constitution of Brazil—that recognize housing as a human right (Government of Brazil 2013). In the context of resettlement, the ordinance makes explicit reference to and recognizes rights that go beyond replacement of lost assets in the context of involuntary displacement by infrastructure works. It affirms that the right to housing, beyond mere physical dwelling, requires measures to restore the social and livelihood conditions of affected families and individuals. The focus on livelihoods along with the connection to the Brazilian federal housing program constitutes one of the key characteristics of the ordinance, as outlined in this section.

Ordinance 317 requires an analysis of alternatives for the main infrastructure development that accounts for potential displacement impacts. The analysis of alternatives must be included in the resettlement plan that is submitted for approval. The ordinance also stresses public participation that includes the participation of affected people in the elaboration of the resettlement plan itself. It requires that the resettlement budget be included in the main project budget. The Ministry of Cities is responsible for approving resettlement plans and, in cases of noncompliance, can withhold disbursements and future investments.

As a condition for the works to be considered complete and delivered, the ordinance requires full implementation of the actions in the resettlement plan.

The main objective of the ordinance with regard to eligibility is the guaranteed right to housing, even in cases of vulnerable tenants. Because it is so closely connected to and influenced by the federal housing program, the ordinance is already geared toward providing housing and public services to people without land or house tenure. One of its limitations, however, is that people can only be beneficiaries of the federal housing program once. A person affected by an infrastructure project that has received a house in the past is not eligible for a compensation package.

In the case of nonvulnerable affected people with tenure, asset replacement may not meet the international standards used by institutions such as the World Bank. Monetary compensation, one avenue of asset replacement, is calculated according to methods and references established by the states, the federal district, or the municipalities, leaving open the possibility of compensation below replacement costs. In other cases, insecure land titles, such as in slum areas in metropolitan regions, still pose a significant implementation challenge. The ordinance also still reserves the right of the state to expropriate property, even if the text emphatically stresses the importance of searching for other solutions. One group that could fall under this category for compensation is medium-sized business owners, especially ones who occupy public lands. Although it is easy to understand the reticence of the municipalities to compensate what they perceive as affluent encroachers on public lands, the actions allowed by the ordinance could result in a reduction of economic activity and employment in an affected area.

One challenge faced when implementing solutions-oriented and policy-compliant resettlement is how to adequately incorporate mitigation and compensation measures beyond the replacement of assets. The need to support existing social networks, livelihood restoration, capacity building, and the adaptation to new living conditions is a challenge that is often inadequately met worldwide by agencies implementing resettlement programs. The development of the Social Work Project in parallel to a resettlement plan, as required by the Ministry of Cities, attempts to address this need, promoting better integration between the specific intervention and measures for its sustainability over time in social and economic terms, both at family and community levels. The Social Work Project aims to ensure synergy between public policies and the infrastructure and services implemented through the resettlement program. This integration is part of Brazil's social and urban inclusion policies, which aim to constitute an integrated approach for addressing urban poverty. Conversely, it might be difficult to increase the participation of civil society organizations as implementation partners in the resettlement process. In Brazil, those organizations tend to have mostly an advocacy and awareness-raising capacity rather than proven implementation skills.

Coverage

An important question in assessing Ordinance 317 against the reality of involuntary displacement in Brazil is the coverage of the regulation. Does it apply to every project involving resettlement in Brazil? The answer is no, but the news is good, nonetheless.

In 2007, the Brazilian federal government created the Growth Acceleration Program (*Programa de Aceleração do Crescimento* or PAC), encompassing a set of economic policies. In 2010, the second Brazilian Growth Acceleration Program (PAC2) was created, with an R$1.59 trillion budget, approximately US$664.96 billion (September 2014 rates). Although the largest single investments in PAC2 are related to energy production in nonurban areas—and notwithstanding the state and interstate transportation projects, which do not come under Ordinance 317's regulatory scope—the majority of PAC2 projects and programs consist of urban service and infrastructure development.

Brazil is an urban country, with 84.4 percent of its population living in urban areas, according to the 2010 official census. Urban transport systems, housing programs, and service infrastructure figure prominently in PAC2. A significant proportion of those projects have their funding channeled through the Ministry of Cities, which is also a natural hub for municipal capacity development. An ordinance issued by the Ministry of Cities, even if applicable only to projects funded through its budget, has a significant reach and trickledown effect that influences capacity and municipal resettlement practices.

Another important factor in assessing the potential reach of Ordinance 317 has to do with the Brazilian federal housing program (*Minha Casa, Minha Vida* or MCMV), which is part of the portfolio of the ministry. Besides being the main government initiative to address the housing gap in Brazil, in practice—if not by force of law—it has become the preferred resettlement compensation strategy in municipality-run projects. Urban upgrading, disaster risk management, transport system development, and other interventions in urban space often lead to the development of a MCMV project so that affected dwellings can be replaced.

Moreover, the use of MCMV projects as the preferred resettlement solution in World Bank– and Inter-American Development Bank–funded urban projects means that the reach of Ordinance 317 is wider than initially expected. Indeed, it also means that the ordinance has direct positive implications for internationally funded development initiatives in Brazilian cities. The coupling of the ordinance with capacity building at the municipal level across the country might represent an effective means of strengthening country systems in a way that is compatible with the World Bank's OP 4.12 and other similar international policies or standards.

Another factor is that infrastructure works in Brazil involve not only significant private sector participation, generally with engineering, procurement, and construction contractors, but also different kinds of public-private partnerships.

Often, some of the activities in the context of resettlement implementation are the responsibility of the private contractor. The new ordinance issued by the Ministry of Cities requires a significant level of capacity development in the public sector, which will lead to a demand for improved engineering, procurement, and construction capacity to deliver services that are in compliance with it. Indirectly, this change in practices could influence resettlement planning and implementation in contexts that do not fall under the regulatory scope of the Ministry of Cities.

Building Municipal Capacity

Notwithstanding the positive potential for development practices, actualizing such a change depends to a great extent on building capacity in thousands of municipal government institutions across Brazil. The World Bank can play a key role in supporting the development of country systems by helping the Ministry of Cities address this challenge.

The Brazilian Ministry of Cities, as well as certain Brazilian municipalities, has already acquired technical and political capacity in involuntary resettlement through the management of complex large-scale resettlement programs in urban areas using in-country resources or funds from the World Bank, the Inter-American Development Bank, and other international donor agencies. Because the quality of resettlement practices has already improved at several levels, many public officials appreciate the value of improved regulations through the publication of Ordinance 317.

The municipalities are relatively independent in the way their administrative structures are organized. Some of the largest municipalities concentrate resettlement planning and management under one of their institutions; others share responsibilities among many secretariats, such as housing, water and sanitation, and education. The challenges faced by municipalities are also heterogeneous, greatly influenced by unique historical urban development processes. Some challenges are common, such as the overall lack of available land located near sites to be resettled. Many Brazilian metropolitan areas face an association between slums, informality, and criminality, compounding the problem. Civil society has become more organized, with nongovernmental organizations and social movements becoming increasingly significant interlocutors of the municipal state.

Even if funding by the Ministry of Cities allows for some federal oversight and regulation, it is the cities that face implementation challenges. Different administrative structures and varying levels of capacity and experience compound the challenge of implementing resettlement according to best practices. Building capacity at the municipal level is the only way to ensure that the new ordinance actually changes the way resettlements are carried out in Brazil, thereby ensuring more equitable treatment for resettled populations.

With the signing of the ordinance by the Brazilian president in July 2013, the World Bank seized an opportunity to leverage efforts and build a more cooperative relationship with the Ministry of Cities. The World Bank's LAC region started working on the development of technical support activities in the form of RAS, through which the World Bank can sell its expertise to the interested country.

The RAS currently in development includes technical support to develop resettlement training for ministry-level officers and municipal civil servants who will be responsible for implementing new urban resettlements in line with Ordinance 317 requirements. At the ministry level, capacity building will probably be carried out face to face with a focus on issues such as training of personnel, budgeting, activity schedules, approval of resettlement plans and responsibilities, and intersectoral coordination. At the municipal level, a partnership between the Ministry of Cities and the World Bank that includes a Brazilian university with experience in long-distance online education is expected. The World Bank's RAS project aims to support the development of course content and to provide technical expertise and support. The beneficiaries will be composed of Brazilian municipalities, with the goal of building capacity in resettlement planning and implementation.

Results and Outcomes

The main case study result has been the publication of Ordinance 317 (Government of Brazil 2013). Although it is too early to evaluate the outcomes of implementing the ordinance, other intermediary results that led to its publication are worthy of mention:

- Dissemination of the World Bank report "Involuntary Resettlement in Brazil: a Review of Policies and Practices" in 2011
- Organization of the International Workshop on Involuntary Resettlement in Brazil 2012, which promoted the dialogue between the Ministry of Cities, international experts, and civil society
- Strengthening of the World Bank's relationship with the Ministry of Cities.

Conclusions

A strong case can be made for changes in how resettlement is implemented in Brazil at the municipal level. Expropriation often pushes the challenges of inadequate housing and informality to new areas, fueling the expansion of existing slums and the occupation of risk areas. Offering adequate solutions avoids future risk and reduces long-term costs associated with urban spatial management. With the strong role currently played by organized society through social and political movements and nongovernmental organizations, more equitable treatment of resettled populations can also help minimize project delays and cost overruns. It might even decrease the likelihood of opposition to future projects.

As a result of the change in regulations made official by Ordinance 317, combined with the large-scale effort in capacity building supported by the World Bank, a cascade effect in resettlement practices in Brazilian urban areas can be expected. As discussed, the ordinance directly applies to projects and programs funded by the Ministry of Cities, which is in charge of most PAC2 urban investments. The changes in resettlement practices triggered by the new involuntary resettlement rules, coupled with an increase in the capacity of municipalities, will influence other ongoing resettlement practices.

The combination of the development of the ordinance with the planned large-scale capacity building, both supported by the World Bank, will likely prove to be a successful case of country systems development even if it does not yet allow for the exclusive use of country systems in lieu of safeguard policies in World Bank-funded projects. The debate around the use of country systems focuses on shared responsibilities and the internalization of social and environmental standards by countries regarding their environmental and social management systems. Although the ordinance receives significant support from the World Bank, it is very appropriate that the development of the ordinance and preparations for its implementation be a Brazilian initiative. The country systems model and agenda asks for more country ownership in environmental and social management. It is very appropriate—perhaps even necessary—for these same country systems to be developed with strong ownership by countries even though World Bank support and political and financial presence are of central importance in pushing for international best practices in resettlement. It is a matter of agency and ownership.

In the context of Brazilian state-run resettlement, in addition to a resettlement plan, regulations require a companion social work plan that articulates resettlement planning with the offer of social services and infrastructure. Such a social work plan makes use of state resources to address themes beyond asset replacement, opening the field for an approach that also takes into account citizenship and human rights. This planning represents a more holistic approach to societal development that goes beyond the limits of any particular project or projects.

With regard to specific operations funded by the World Bank, the new ordinance simplifies dialogues, as OP 4.12 and Ordinance 317 can now be compared and used side by side in the social management of projects. In many ways, the ordinance is an instrument resembling OP 4.12. It introduces a synergy that works toward better practices in joint initiatives.

Although they do not fully comply with World Bank policy, the changes to resettlement regulations and practices in Brazil represent a very effective example of how country systems can be strengthened with the support of international financing institutions and donor agencies (see boxes 2.1 and 2.2). A number of international agreements support the increased use of country systems. Their use must be operationalized in a way that protects people and the environment affected by development projects. The Brazilian case, as embodied in the issuance of Ordinance 317, as well as all actions that preceded and may follow it, could prove to be a milestone in this regard. (See boxes 2.3 and 2.4.)

Box 2.1 Contributing Factors to Passing of Ordinance 317

"The country was ready. The result was made possible by the sum of several small things:

- We already had a solid relation with the Secretariat of Housing of the ministry.
- It was the right moment, with the mega events and the social context of the country.
- We had the right entry point.
- It was a government sensitive to social issues.
- We had the professional and personal relationships in place."

Source: Sameh Naguib Wahba, LAC sector leader for the Sustainable Development Department at the time of creation of the nonlending technical assistance, the report on resettlement practices in Brazil, and the International Workshop.

Box 2.2 How Do You Think This Experience Could Be Reproduced in Other Countries?

"One could analyze the [World] Bank's portfolio in a country and ask: 'Where are we [as] a stakeholder?'

After you identify an entry point, you identify your champion. And you enable local institutions to develop on their terms. You engage by

- Being an uninterested party (without an agenda);
- Looking for a way to solve their problems, not ours;
- Being innovative;
- Listening, listening, and listening before you say anything;
- Developing personal and institutional relations with your stakeholders.

This kind of activity represents a small investment for the potential return, if compared to projects. There is a risk it won't work, but if it works, it yields a much greater return."

Source: Fabio Pittaluga, Senior Social Development Specialist, LAC, Task Team Leader (TTL) of the International Workshop on Involuntary Displacement in Brazil and TTL of reimbursable advisory services in preparation to help the Ministry of Cities in Brazil build capacity in the municipalities.

Box 2.3 Summary of Innovative Practices

The main innovative practice highlighted in this case study involved combining factors in a way that promoted policy development with minimal cost to the World Bank:

- Use of an existing World Bank portfolio in a given sector as leverage to support the development of sectoral policy that is in line with the World Bank's goals
- Use of the World Bank's convening power to help bring together government and civil society stakeholders to discuss development of a new sectoral policy

box continues next page

Box 2.3 Summary of Innovative Practices *(continued)*

- Support of the client in resolving its problems according to its own agenda, instead of pursuing the World Bank's agenda
- Use of World Bank instruments, such as nontechnical assistance and reimbursable advisory services, to support the client's objectives before and after publication of a new sectoral policy.

Box 2.4 Key Lessons Learned

- *Identify the entry point.*
  - Examine the World Bank's portfolio in the country. Where does the World Bank have projects and established relationships?
  - Where is there already enough capacity to support an advanced dialogue?
  - Where is there a problem for which the client is searching for a solution?
  - Where is the World Bank a stakeholder?
- *Build on existing relationships—both institutional and personal.*
  Give close attention to the choice of people involved. A champion was identified in the Ministry of Cities, and the consultants selected to support the development of the ordinance had already worked for the ministry, bringing their own relationships to the process.
- *Leverage existing capacity.*
  Using in-country resources or funds from the World Bank, the Inter-American Development Bank, and other international sources, the Brazilian Ministry of Cities and particularly many Brazilian municipalities had existing capacity directly resulting from experience with managing complex large-scale resettlement in urban areas. One considerable challenge is addressing capacity needs in a large number of municipalities with different administrative structures and levels of experience.
- *Engage stakeholders.*
  Engaging stakeholders is a lengthy process, but one that makes an initiative politically feasible. The Government of Brazil's (2013) Ministry of Cities' Ordinance 317 became official in July 2013, after a two-year process of public consultation and debates among critical stakeholders, including local governments, private sector companies, and the Council of Cities—an urban policy body with representatives from civil society and the public and private sector. The World Bank had to stay the course with regard to the development of the dialogue and accept that local political processes are what ultimately determine whether change will be viable.
- *Follow through and follow up.*
  Aim at milestones that advance the process. Use different World Bank tools to follow through. In the case study, the World Bank financed a study of involuntary resettlement practices and policies in Brazil. The study was followed by an international workshop, which

box continues next page

Box 2.4 Key Lessons Learned *(continued)*

may lead to a project in the form of reimbursable advisory services (RAS) to help Brazil build capacity in its municipalities. The first two activities were financed through World Bank–funded nonlending technical assistance; the RAS would be nationally financed.

• *Country systems need country ownership.*

Country systems must be developed with strong ownership by the countries—even if World Bank support and political and financial presence are centrally important in pushing for international best practices in resettlement or other social and environmental practices.

References

Government of Brazil. 2013. "Ordinance 317, Ministry of Cities." Portaria n° 317, de 18 de julho de 2013 [in Portuguese], http://pesquisa.in.gov.br/imprensa/jsp/visualiza /index.jsp?data=19/07/2013&jornal=1&pagina=42&totalArquivos=144.

World Bank. 2012. "Nonlending Technical Assistance (NLTA) on Strengthening and Transforming Institutions for Management of Land Acquisition and Resettlement and Rehabilitation in Partnership with the Ministry of Rural Development of India." Completion Note (April), World Bank, Washington, DC.

CHAPTER 3

Relocation of Informal Urban Settlements: Examples from India and Mauritania

Mumbai Urban Transport Project in India

Rationale for Case Study Selection

Land acquisition and resettlement are dominant issues in Indian cities because a large share of the urban population lives in slums or as encroachers. In the past, these issues were a major barrier to urban and infrastructure development. The Mumbai Urban Transport Project (MUTP) was a landmark effort because it was the first attempt to resettle a large number of slum dwellers in an urban area. It involved the displacement of 17,572 households—about 100,000 people—as well as the removal of 1,822 commercial establishments of varying sizes, including 566 shops with floor areas exceeding 225 square feet or 20.8 square meters, and about 100 religious and community properties. MUTP remains the largest urban resettlement and rehabilitation (R&R) project funded by the World Bank, as well as the largest R&R project in India to date.

The case study highlights two innovative dimensions of this groundbreaking resettlement program:

- Participatory approaches to large-scale slum enumeration and resettlement planning with the assistance of local nongovernmental organizations (NGOs)
- Capacity building of the resettlement implementation agency.

The case study summarizes three additional elements in the resettlement program that are of particular interest: gender inclusion approaches, grievance redress mechanisms, and transparency initiatives.

In addition to materials available in the project files and on the Internet—including resettlement reports, implementation completion reports, inspection panel reports, and articles—the case study draws heavily from the Innovation note, "Urban Resettlement for the Mumbai Urban Transport Project" which was produced as a collaboration between the task team and the resettlement implementation agency (World Bank and Ministry of Finance of India 2012). It also builds on the *Guidance Note on Urban Resettlement*, which was prepared under the MUTP by the World Bank and the Government of Maharashtra (2009).

Project Background

The contents of this section are largely based on excerpts from the Innovation note, "Urban Resettlement for the Mumbai Urban Transport Project" (World Bank and Ministry of Finance of India 2012).

Project Development Context

Known for its economic dynamism, traffic jams, and vast slums, Mumbai is the financial capital of India and home to about 12 million people. Seven million people live in 3,000 slums across the city, encroaching on vital public lands and obstructing infrastructure, including roads, airports, drains, stations, and markets. Slums have also spread to private lands because of the Urban Land Ceilings Act of 1976, which restricted the use of private land holdings above 500 square meters. Affordable housing is a challenge, and much needed amenities are often out of reach to many, pushing poor migrants to settle in slums. Public transport plays a dominant role in the Mumbai Metropolitan Region, with rail and bus services carrying 88 percent of the region's motorized personal trips. Suburban rail services carry more than 6 million passengers per day, and buses transport more than 4.5 million passengers per day—60 percent of whom transfer to rail. Despite its crucial role, the public transport system in Mumbai is faced with formidable problems, including congestion, limited infrastructure, pollution, traffic management, and safety issues. These problems pose a major challenge to Mumbai's prospects for remaining India's top investment destination.

Economic reforms initiated in the 1990s created new opportunities and triggered competition among Indian cities to attract private investments. Cities offering better infrastructure, services, management settings, and labor forces were more likely to succeed as new economic magnets. The urban transport sector was unprepared to deal with issues that accompany fast urbanization—namely, insufficient and inefficient public transport, rapid growth in motorization, heavy traffic congestion, poor road networks and traffic safety, high transport-related pollution, and weak institutional arrangements in metropolitan regions. The economic boom of the following decade brought unprecedented pressure on urban civic infrastructure on a scale that could undermine growth and transformation. Against this backdrop, the Maharashtra government embarked on the "Transform Mumbai" initiative, which comprised several projects.

The MUTP was launched in 2002 with the aim of improving urban transport services in Mumbai by reducing overcrowding on trains, reducing travel times for more than 6 million daily commuters, enhancing road transport connectivity, modernizing traffic management and control systems, improving transportation planning, and resettling 100,000 slum dwellers who lived in the vicinity of railway tracks and roadways (box 3.1).

Box 3.1 Mumbai Urban Transport Project at a Glance

The project development objective was to facilitate urban economic growth and improve quality of life by fostering the development of an efficient and sustainable urban transport system, including the promotion of effective institutions in the Mumbai metropolitan region.

Component 1—Rail Transport: Improvement in capacity and performance of the suburban rail network through the provision of rail track additions; signaling systems; increased power; new rail cars, among other enhancements; and technical assistance

Component 2—Road-Based Transport: Selected area traffic control and traffic management infrastructure schemes (Municipal Corporation of Greater Mumbai), procurement of 644 buses by the Bombay Electricity and Suburban Transport Corporation, and road widening to facilitate two east-west links—Jogeshwari Vikhroli Link Road and Santa Cruz–Chembur Link Road (Maharashtra State Roads Development Corporation)

Component 3—Resettlement and Rehabilitation: Provision of alternative housing and services for resettlement and rehabilitation of project-affected persons by the Mumbai Metropolitan Region Development Authority. (The cost of this component was US$92 million.)

Project Implementation: 2002–11

Project Cost and Financing: US$1.1 billion (total)—US$463 million International Bank for Reconstruction and Development loan, US$92 million International Development Association credit, and counterpart financing of US$568 million by the government of India.

Photo 3.1 illustrates the housing situation for project-affected persons along the railway tracks (a) before resettlement and (b) after resettlement.

Multiple agencies implemented the project, with the Mumbai Metropolitan Region Development Authority (MMRDA) playing a coordinating role. In addition to the government of India and the state government of Maharashtra, participating agencies included the Mumbai Rail Vikas Corporation, the Municipal Corporation of Greater Mumbai, the Bombay Electricity and Suburban Transport Corporation, the Maharashtra State Roads Development Corporation (MSRDC), and the Traffic Police of Mumbai.

Resettlement Policy Context

Before MUTP, the government of Maharashtra did not have a resettlement policy in its regulatory framework. There was limited institutional capacity at the state or city level for handling large-scale involuntary resettlement operations. In 2000, as part of project preparation, the state government developed an R&R policy that provided guidelines for compensation and assistance to project-affected persons (PAPs) when resettlement could not be avoided.

The policy was formulated in line with the World Bank's policy on involuntary resettlement. It recommended that each project-affected household be fully compensated for loss of land and assets and that all affected households, including landowners, tenants, and squatters, be provided with free replacement

Photo 3.1 Mumbai Urban Transport Project—Before and After Resettlement

a. Before resettlement

b. After resettlement

Source: World Bank Office, New Delhi, India.

housing or commercial premises of 225 square feet. Affected shopkeepers and residential landowners were offered the opportunity to buy additional floor space in proportion to their loss up to an additional 525 square feet on payment of an approved cost. Landowners in the affected areas were also offered transfer of development rights (TDR) or adjustments to the allowable floor space index

(FSI) in lieu of cash compensation for loss of land. They could apply TDR or FSI to properties elsewhere on the local market.

In addition to compensation for loss of land and assets, the policy required that PAPs be provided with relocation assistance and post-resettlement support. In the case of the MUTP, this included the registration and training of housing societies for the management of buildings in resettlement townships in the central districts of Mumbai; one-time financial assistance for maintaining buildings and managing community affairs; environmental management; common facilities for women and children; and basic services, such as schools, transportation, water, internal roads, and street lighting. It also included a number of measures to strengthen income restoration activities in the resettlement colonies with a particular focus on youth and women.

Providing free housing to more than 100,000 people within the city of Mumbai required the construction of several fully serviced resettlement townships, which demanded enormous financial resources. Recognizing the challenge, the Maharashtra state government encouraged private sector participation in the resettlement program by offering additional development rights or FSI to private developers willing to pay for the resettlement of slum dwellers. The economics of slum resettlement and related urban renewal slowly gained currency as developers learned to convert TDR and FSI into profitable investments in the Mumbai real estate market. (See box 3.2.)

Box 3.2 Transfer of Development Rights

Transfer of development rights (TDR) is a certificate from the Municipal Corporation of Greater Mumbai (MCGM) that a property owner receives in exchange for land surrendered for public purposes. Providing a definition of TDR, Rule 34 of the Development Control Regulation (DCR) of Greater Bombay, 1991, states, "In certain circumstances, the development potential of a plot of land may be separated from the land itself and may be made available to the owner of the land in the form of Transferable Development Rights. These rights may be made available and be subject to the Regulations in Appendix VII of DCR." TDR is the development potential of the land, suspended because of the reservation or acquisition of land by the government of Maharashtra for public purposes.

Under the TDR policy, landowners receive compensation in the form of a Development Right Certificate (detached development rights equal to the development potential of a land plot) for surrendering land to the government for purposes such as widening a road, creating a park, or rehabilitating slum dwellings. TDR allows the government to avoid cumbersome procedures to acquire land at heavy compensation, and it enables the government to compensate the landowner with a TDR certificate under which the development potential of the land is detached from the land taken or reserved. The landowner is compensated by additional floor space index (FSI) that can be used on some other land above the normal FSI permitted in relation to that piece of land.

box continues next page

Box 3.2 **Transfer of Development Rights** *(continued)*

TDR is a negotiable instrument that can be bought and sold or can be used by the land-owner for development of another land plot to the north of the surrendered plot with additional FSI above that approved under DCR. Most TDRs are generated from the redevelopment of slums, initiated by the Municipal Corporation of Greater Mumbai and the Mumbai Metropolitan Region Development Authority (MMRDA). In the case of slum resettlement, developers are offered additional TDR and floor space index of between 1.5 and 2.5 times the area created, which can be used to develop other properties at a profit. One square foot of TDR can cost about Rs 4,000 (US$60–70) in Mumbai, depending on its location. Some trace the origin of the idea of TDR to the American zoning ordinance first introduced in New York City in 1916.

Land Tenure, Resettlement Planning, and Implementation Context

While most project-affected households did not have formal ownership of their properties, a number of them benefited from a semilegal status as leaseholders, tenants, or notified slum dwellers. A large proportion—about 10,000 of the 17,572 residential project-affected households—lived in unsafe conditions in informal settlements along the railway tracks and generally welcomed the relocation from the harsh living conditions. Unlike the railway PAPs, the road-affected PAPs were more socioeconomically diverse and geographically dispersed. They included land-owners, leaseholders, and operators of large commercial establishments that were tied to their locations, with established incomes and social networks. They objected to being categorized as slum dwellers and were opposed to relocation.

The MUTP resettlement policy provided two main resettlement options for slum dwellers:

- The "Township/Sites and Services" option was a project developed by the resettlement agency on a greenfield site owned by the agency, with a fully developed 25-square-meter plot allocated one year ahead of the anticipated relocation date. The agency developed some of the land in the township for higher-income housing of non-PAPs and for commercial activities and sold plots at market price for development by private developers of commercial estates and high-income housing, actions which helped recover project costs. A PAP who chose this option was entitled to monetary compensation equaling the replacement cost of the shelter at the time of the baseline survey so that a new structure could be rebuilt on the serviced plot.
- The much more common "Resettlement Colony" option, also known as the "Slum Redevelopment Scheme," involved multistoried buildings built under the supervision of the resettlement agency for the sole purpose of allocation to slum dwellers. The typical resettlement benefit allocated to slum dwellers was a tenement of 225 square feet in a multistoried building within the resettlement colony.

The resettlement of slum dwellers from horizontally spread-out slums with limited informal community services to modern multistory buildings in fully serviced resettlement colonies raised a number of challenges because of the inexperience of PAPs in managing formal housing and its surroundings. Although relocated households could retain access to sources of urban incomes and employment, they had to get accustomed to very different living conditions. Without adequate support to new residents, resettlement buildings ran the risk of turning into vertical slums. Even with transitional support from the resettlement implementation agency and from community NGOs, management gaps remained, affecting living conditions in the resettlement sites. Issues such as inadequate access to transportation services, schools, and hospitals; the need for civic provisions for waste management; and requirements for maintenance of common facilities such as open spaces, lighting and lifts, internal roads, and drainage posed sustainability risks.

Planning and implementing such an ambitious urban resettlement operation was not without its difficulties, particularly with regard to resettling PAPs affected by the road corridors. In addition to the direct costs of compensation and livelihood restoration for project-affected households, insufficient engagement with certain groups of PAPs resulted in substantial construction delays.

> During the MUTP implementation, for example, problems arose with affected shopkeepers because they were dissatisfied with the R&R package, which was mainly intended for affected residents and was based on a replacement apartment in a resettlement colony. These problems arose because shopkeepers had not been adequately identified or consulted with at the baseline stage, and no specific package had been designed for them. The negotiation with shopkeepers took time, amongst others because the government of Maharashtra was initially unwilling to make the R&R package more flexible and accommodate the shopkeeper's needs. These delays had huge implications on the cost of infrastructure, with contractors unable to work, as well as more economic implications, with for example longer periods of works impacting traffic and safety. (World Bank and Government of Maharashtra 2009, 6)

In 2004, in response to four requests for an investigation on behalf of several hundred PAPs from Jogeshwari Vikhroli Link Road (JVLR) and Santa Cruz–Chembur Link Road (SCLR), a World Bank Inspection Panel case was opened. In 2005, an investigation was conducted on the resettlement process carried out for the project. The requesters mainly questioned the adequacy of resettlement options for shopkeepers, the suitability and quality of resettlement sites, information disclosure, and the grievance redress process. The panel reported its findings in December 2005, after which World Bank management prepared an action plan in cooperation with the government of Maharashtra to improve the quality and outcomes of the resettlement processes. The disbursement of the resettlement component of the project was suspended in March 2006, and a range of remedial actions were initiated. Some of the key issues addressed as part of the remedial actions included the following:

- Negotiating with the shopkeepers about their resettlement
- Ensuring post-resettlement sustainability
- Improving basic services in the resettlement colonies

- Strengthening consultations with PAPs
- Streamlining information disclosure and the grievance redress process
- Enhancing institutional capacity for the management of the resettlement
- Updating and strengthening resettlement data management, reporting, and implementation procedures.

The implementation of these remedial actions resulted in progressive improvement in the manner in which MMRDA planned and implemented resettlement measures. Sustained efforts to engage with PAPs to listen to and resolve their resettlement issues on the basis of alternate and flexible approaches enabled the agency to gradually restore trust. The project was closed after four extensions in 2011, and a final report by World Bank management was delivered to the World Bank Board of Directors in 2013 following the successful completion of the corrective action plan.

Thematic Analysis

Resettlement activities were a key component of the project because of the large number of people being resettled. This component of the project supported measures to improve the policy framework and institutional and implementation arrangements for resettlement; it also provided funding for the resettlement activities. The first step in the process was to develop resettlement plans. To this end, a key decision made by the government was entrusting the assignment to local NGOs.

Participatory Slum Enumeration and Resettlement Planning

Collaboration with NGOs in resettlement activities was not a common approach in India. MUTP hired NGOs with extensive experience working with slum communities in Mumbai to assist with the resettlement of slum dwellers, including preparing and implementing resettlement plans. Relying on local NGOs as a channel of engagement was considered an innovative way to connect with urban slum communities.

As a foundation for the development of resettlement plans, community-based NGOs carried out baseline socioeconomic surveys and contributed to the preparation of resettlement implementation plans for various subprojects under MUTP. The baseline socioeconomic surveys helped to define who was eligible for compensation, and they provided the basis for the allocation of accommodations on the resettlement sites. The surveys promoted a community-based, women-centered, participatory approach to resettlement. PAPs were consulted in different stages of designing, planning, and implementing the resettlement program. Photo 3.2 shows an example of a Flat Occupation Certificate for resettled PAPs.

A key highlight of this participatory process was extensive PAP consultations conducted by project officials to explore negotiated resettlement options for the affected large- and medium-size shops along the east-west link roads (JVLR and SCLR) undertaken under MUTP. As a result, MMRDA was able to resolve

Photo 3.2 Inheritance Nomination Deposited by the New Flat Owners with the Housing Cooperative. All Flat Owners Have Their Flat Occupation Certificates.

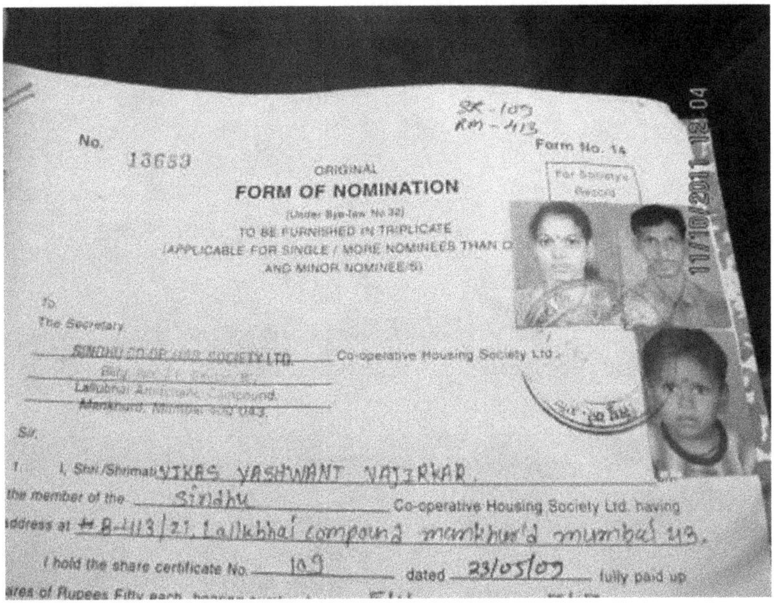
No. 13683

ORIGINAL

FORM OF NOMINATION

Form No. 14

To

The Secretary

Co-operative Housing Society Ltd.

Sir,

I, Shri /Shrimati VIKAS YASHWANT ... the member of the Sindhu Co-operative Housing Society Ltd. having address at ... Lallubhai compound mankhurd mumbai 43.

I hold the share certificate No. 109 dated 23/05/07 fully paid up

Source: World Bank Office, New Delhi, India.

challenging relocation issues with several commercial and residential PAP associations by offering a range of resettlement options that included in situ redevelopment enabling the PAPs to retain their locational advantage. Some 444 families living in multistory residential blocks demanded to be resettled within close vicinity of their original location. About 120 of them opted for private redevelopment schemes; MMRDA took responsibility for building new residential blocks to resettle the rest of the families. Similarly, about 380 shopkeepers affected by JVLR, including legal shop owners, were resettled in a shopping mall established at Powai. Of 550 large- and medium-size shops, about 150 opted for a private redevelopment scheme, whereas about 100 opted for relocation to a nearby resettlement building.

The participatory approach helped to reestablish a number of religious and community structures, including mosques, temples, shrines, and welfare centers, away from the roads. The custodians of these facilities were provided with construction costs along with an alternative site (which required resettlement of additional slum households) to rebuild their facilities. Photos 3.3 and 3.4 provide illustrations of a mosque and welfare center and of a shopping mall that were rebuilt as part of the resettlement program.

The involvement of NGOs in collecting baseline data in informal settlements, proactive consultation with PAPs, forming PAP women groups, and providing them with mobilization support for shifting, helped to ensure that the relocation of slum dwellers to new resettlement colonies was largely peaceful and free from incidents.

Photo 3.3 Reconstruction of Mosque and Welfare Center along SCLR

a. Mosque wall along SCLR

b. Welfare center along SCLR

Source: World Bank Office, New Delhi, India.
Note: SCLR = Santa Cruz–Chembur Link Road.

Photo 3.4 Powai Shopping Mall along JVLR

Source: World Bank Office, New Delhi, India.
Note: JVLR = Jogeshwari Vikhroli Link Road.

Nevertheless, the lesson learned from this approach was that even NGOs with many years of grassroots experience in local informal settlements might not have sufficient capacity at the outset of a project to handle large-scale resettlement planning that involves complex baseline studies. In some instances, there were gaps in data quality and complaints regarding eligibility. Therefore, over the life of the project, MUTP expanded its in-house capacity for social mobilization and worked with NGOs to strengthen their capabilities and streamline their role in the resettlement process.

Capacity Building of the Resettlement Implementation Agency

At the outset of the project, MMRDA, the coordinating implementation agency, did not have sufficient capacity to design and implement a resettlement program of such unprecedented magnitude in India. The World Bank's safeguard policy requirement on involuntary resettlement prompted the state government to adopt a new resettlement policy. Because the project was one of the first of its kind handled by the agency, there was a steep learning curve. The capacity building of MMRDA took place over the life of the project. Despite experiencing initial challenges and roadblocks in handling resettlement, the agency developed substantial capacity that extended beyond the life of MUTP.

Over time, the agency created a permanent Social Development Unit (SDU) to manage resettlement impacts of various projects in the city. The SDU in MMRDA is headed by a chief officer who reports to the metropolitan commissioner. The chief officer is assisted by several officers working with the SDU including land acquisition officers, engineers, and social development assistants. During the implementation phase, a special Post-Resettlement Support Unit was created to plan and implement post-resettlement activities, including (a) PAP housing cooperative registration; (b) management training; (c) provision of services such as water and sanitation, schools, and inner street lights; and (d) economic empowerment of resettled women. The SDU has cells looking after livelihoods, human development index, and R&R management. The agency has reestablished the MUTP's grievance redress mechanisms for its new project, MUTP-2B, which is funded from its own resources.

The World Bank's task team worked with MMRDA to enhance its resettlement capabilities throughout the life of the project. As a result of the collaboration between the government of Maharashtra, the World Bank, and outside experts, the World Bank published the "Guidance Note on Urban Resettlement" (World Bank and Government of Maharashtra 2009). The publication provides specific guidance for complex urban-to-urban resettlement operations related to infrastructure projects in large cities, with a particular focus on impoverished areas and slums. Special attention is given to "the difficult issue of income restoration, including for business owners, as well as the longer-term issue of sustainability of new (often multistory) communities of resettled people" (World Bank and Government of Maharashtra 2009, 8). The guidebook was developed on the basis of consultations with civil society organizations that were held by the World Bank in India in September 2006 and on an international resettlement workshop convened by the World Bank a week later in Thailand, in which a number of Indian government agencies and experts participated. The preparation of the guidebook was supported by additional workshops in 2008 that enabled other Indian cities—Hyderabad, Chennai, and Delhi—to share their experiences with urban resettlement programs.

The MUTP resettlement process has become a worldwide example of successfully resettling unprecedented numbers of project-affected people, mostly slum dwellers, in a densely populated urban area and, as a result, improving peoples' lives. Lessons learned have equipped the MMRDA to effectively deal with resettlement challenges in other infrastructure projects. In recognition of its capacity and experience, the government of Maharashtra has designated MMRDA as the key government agency for managing resettlement operations for several new infrastructure projects in Mumbai, including Metro, Monorail, and MUTP-2A. The agency has mainstreamed the application of the MUTP's resettlement policy to resettlement activities beyond the project. It has applied the MUTP's resettlement entitlement framework to all of its resettlement projects and has expanded the MUTP's post-resettlement support strategy to all resettlement sites, irrespective of their funding sources. MMRDA is now recognized in India and abroad for its innovative approach to resettlement.

Other Innovative Approaches

This section is based mainly on excerpts from the MUTP Implementation Completion Report (World Bank 2011).

Gender Inclusion Approaches. Although MUTP did not prepare a stand-alone gender action plan, gender and social development considerations were integrated into the overall project design and implementation process. The resettlement baseline survey was designed to generate gender-disaggregated data on the age, sex, and income of affected persons. This collection of data helped to identify women-headed and vulnerable households that could then be given preferential treatment in the offering of alternative housing. Each resettlement building had a women's center, providing a forum for activities for women, including self-help, thrift, and savings groups. Women workers who lost their supplementary incomes had access to microcredit groups, and some were given vocational training. Over 10,000 women were engaged in these group activities. MMRDA formed an industrial cooperative that provided income opportunities to approximately 1,000 women. Photos 3.5 and 3.6 provide examples of a women-led cooperative bakery and of an apartment in a resettlement building.

Resettled women expressed greater satisfaction with their new homes than did men because they appreciated the increased privacy and enhanced personal security. Each building had a children's center with preschool and day care services, enabling women to engage in productive activities. Women's participation in the management of the resettlement buildings was ensured by reserving membership for women in the housing cooperative executive committees. With the support of partner NGOs, a number of women formed community police groups that focused on domestic violence issues, marital conflicts, and financial transactions among resettled PAPs—particularly those

Photo 3.5 Women Running Their Cooperative Bakery

Source: World Bank Office, New Delhi, India.

Photo 3.6 A Resettled Woman in Her New Home

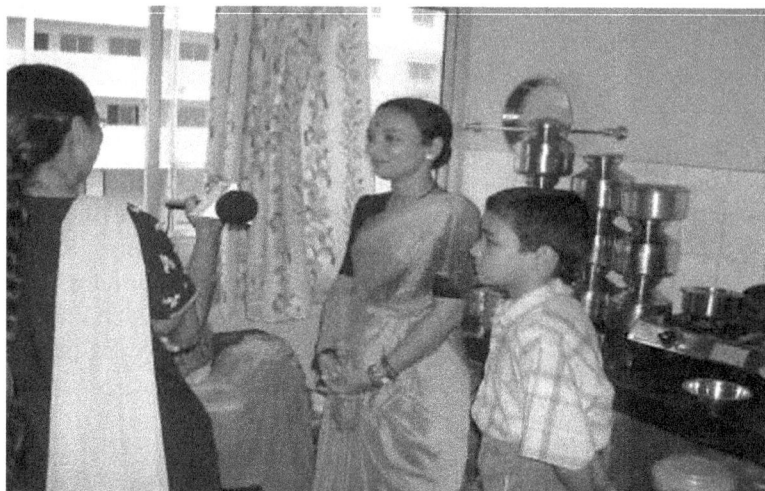

Source: World Bank Office, New Delhi, India.

involving female recipients. The Mumbai police department formally recognized the role of such groups. The 11-member community police committee has seven female members, who have all been issued identification cards as social police officers by the Mumbai police. Women's groups have played a key role in rebuilding lost social capital and in resolving conflicts and differences in the resettlement buildings and colonies as a whole.

Grievance Redress Mechanisms. At the appraisal stage, the project established a two-stage grievance redress process, which was streamlined during implementation. The grievance redress committees—field and senior levels—handled complaints and grievances from PAPs. The field-level grievance redress committee considered individual grievances, and a senior-level grievance redress committee considered appeals against field-level grievance redress committee decisions. Independent, respected citizens not associated with project implementation administered complaints. The field-level grievance redress committee heard and resolved 3,704 cases, of which 1,169 received favorable verdicts. The senior-level grievance redress committee resolved 902 cases, of which 294 cases received favorable verdicts. An independent resettlement impact assessment study carried out in 2007–08 (TISS 2008) recorded a high degree of PAP satisfaction with the grievance redress process.

During the project implementation phase, the government of Maharashtra established an independent monitoring panel composed of eminent citizens, including a former chief secretary of the state as its chairman, a senior advocate, a senior journalist, a former vice chancellor of the university in Mumbai, and a noted academic. The panel considered group complaints and policy-related issues. It also visited resettlement sites with officials, inspected the sites, interacted with the people to understand their concerns, and recommended remedial actions to be taken by MMRDA, which were submitted in the action taken report. An independent study (TISS 2008) emphasized the positive contributions made by the panel to the monitoring of resettlement implementation and of addressing PAPs' concerns.

The appeals procedure was streamlined and incorporated into the MUTP R&R implementation manual. The grievance redress mechanism process was also circulated among PAPs. House allotment letters informed the PAPs about the grievance redress procedures, which allowed a person to file a complaint and then submit evidence within five working days. The independent monitoring panel was assigned the responsibility of stepping in where group interests or policy matters were involved. The single-member grievance redress committees were assigned the task of hearing and resolving cases pertaining to eligibility for entitlements (to alternative houses or shops).

In addition, MMRDA established a system for hearing and addressing a wide range of grievances, including post-resettlement issues, with specific weekdays set aside for this purpose. PAPs had access to these grievance hearings through MMRDA's chief R&R office. They could also ask the independent monitoring panel to resolve broader policy issues, including those involving group complaints. To address people's complaints in resettlement sites, MMRDA constituted decentralized grievance committees in five key resettlement colonies, managed by its engineers. Under this arrangement, MMRDA engineers periodically held grievance hearings in resettlement sites and took remedial actions. Complainants whose claims were declined by the grievance redress committees retained the option of seeking recourse in court. MMRDA dealt with about 50 court cases filed by PAPs regarding resettlement issues.

Transparency Initiatives. MMRDA disclosed the resettlement action plan, summaries of resettlement implementation plans for specific subprojects, and lists of eligible PAPs on its website. The agency also regularly disclosed key resettlement documents on its website, such as the R&R implementation manual, a grievance redress brochure, resettlement procedures in the event of a failure in negotiations with shopkeepers, procedures for retaining partially affected structures, procedures for implementing the balance of resettlement activities for the road over bridges removed from MUTP as part of project restructuring, and other notifications. MMRDA ran a public information center out of its office. The Right to Information Act of 2005 further strengthened transparency and accountability practices in MUTP. In response to this law, MMRDA designated public information officers for resettlement and disclosed public information officer contact names and phone numbers on its website.

Results and Outcomes
By the end of MUTP, MMRDA had developed about 30 new (often multistory) resettlement townships or colonies for slum dwellers in the City of Mumbai, including 13 sites earmarked for MUTP PAPs.[1] Through World Bank loan

closures, all but six residential households and all but 40 shopkeepers had been resettled, including those who opted for non-MUTP slum rehabilitation schemes, partial retention of structures, or in situ redevelopment schemes. All religious structures, except for three, had been relocated, and legal proceedings had been initiated for the remaining cases.

In addition, the implementation of a post-resettlement support strategy ensured the registration of PAP housing societies, provided them with technical and financial assistance, and enabled them to responsibly manage their assets and surroundings. This strategy included exit indicators that enabled the handover of management responsibilities to PAP housing societies. At the closure of MUTP, 95 percent of cooperatives had been registered and trained to responsibly self-manage their affairs. Resettled people had slowly gained confidence in accepting the change and managing their own affairs.[2]

Conclusions

Overall, MUTP presents a good practice case study for urban resettlement because the project introduced a number of innovative practices that were subsequently applied to other urban projects in India. The project had a demonstration effect for other large urban resettlement operations else-where. Some of these innovative practices and lessons learned were captured in the "Innovation Note on Urban Resettlement for the MUTP" (World Bank and Ministry of Finance of India 2012) and are summarized below. (See boxes 3.3 and 3.4.)

Box 3.3 Summary of Innovative Practices

Good practices documented in the case study include the use of self-administered socio-economic baseline surveys for resettlement (with the assistance of local nongovernmental organizations) and the successful capacity building of Mumbai's municipal resettlement authority. Other innovative practices included the following:

- The development of mechanisms and practices for the participation of affected people, through consultation, participation, and engagement with civil society organizations
- The recourse of market-based solutions such as transfer of development rights as a tradable benefit in lieu of land compensation for resettlement operations in urban slums
- The provision of free alternative housing with title, which had an empowering effect on resettled households that acquired new social status and gained wider access to employment in the formal sector
- The use of periodic socioeconomic monitoring and evaluation to measure the adequacy and effectiveness of resettlement solutions and to undertake course correction if required to fill gaps.

Box 3.4 Key Lessons Learned

- Transition from an administrative compensation approach toward a win-win negotiated approach by the government minimized opposition from several groups of project-affected persons (PAPs). In some cases, the government went beyond policy alternatives to resolve resettlement issues.
- Introducing entitlements and market-based solutions contributed to the success of the Mumbai Urban Transport Project (MUTP). The provision of free alternative housing with titles had an empowering effect on PAPs who acquired new social status and gained wider access to formal sector employment. The market solution of offering transfer of development rights as a tradable benefit in lieu of land compensation provided more options for legal owners to recover losses.
- Effective consultations and communication with PAPs helped with several issues, including checking misinformation, building trust, and negotiating resettlement options.
- An effective grievance redress mechanism allowed the timely resolution of entitlement-related complaints and reduced transaction costs for both affected people and authorities. The independent monitoring panel enhanced trust and accountability by monitoring the resettlement process with field visits and by resolving complaints.
- Assessing the capacity of nongovernmental organizations and understanding their approaches is key to effectively engaging them in resettlement activities and avoiding task overload and inefficiencies. The MUTP showed that even nongovernmental organizations with significant experience might need capacity strengthening.
- A lack of adequate synchronization of resettlement activities with civil works caused significant time and cost overruns during the MUTP. Prior to the commencement of civil works, substantial land acquisition and resettlement should always be completed.
- Interagency coordination issues posed a serious challenge to smooth implementation of urban projects. The delays faced by the Mumbai Metropolitan Region Development Authority (MMRDA) in finalizing designs for the Santa Cruz–Chembur Link Road Over Bridges with Indian Railways and the ongoing negotiations between MMRDA and the Municipal Corporation of Greater Mumbai regarding the fuller integration of resettlement sites into the urban services network illustrate this point.
- Periodic socioeconomic monitoring and evaluation helped to measure the adequacy and effectiveness of resettlement solutions and allowed course correction to fill gaps to be undertaken when required. Following the 2008 impact evaluation, the MMRDA took several remedial measures to improve the quality of the post-resettlement support strategy.
- The MUTP experience demonstrated that the use of transit resettlement should be avoided to minimize uncertainties with regard to permanent resettlement and to minimize risks associated with people living in low-quality temporary facilities.
- At permanent resettlement sites, common amenities should be integrated into overall layouts and designs, including essential common facilities to be developed prior to relocation of affected people.
- Estate management should be integrated into resettlement planning and implementation to ensure a smooth transition to new resettlement sites.

Sources: World Bank and Government of Maharashtra 2009; World Bank 2013a.

Urban Development Project in Nouakchott, Mauritania

Rationale for Case Study Selection

The population of Nouakchott, the capital city of Mauritania, has grown at least fivefold over the past 30–40 years as a consequence of successive droughts and conflicts in rural areas and rapid urbanization. The city's population, estimated at about 560,000 in 2000, is now more than 700,000—the city is the largest in the Sahara. Many recent arrivals have settled in city slums, locally known as *kebbe*, or in slightly better quality unauthorized city settlements known as *gazra*.

Over the past 20 years, the government of Mauritania has tried to relocate slum dwellers to formally designated urban expansion zones. Nouakchott contains six slums with a total population of approximately 250,000–300,000. The El Mina slum, with an estimated 40,000 inhabitants, is the largest *kebbe* in Nouakchott. This densely settled area is located immediately to the southwest of the city center and has significant economic potential. It is well served by major arterial roads, including the main road to the city's deep-sea port. In 2000, the government decided to restructure and upgrade this slum as a pilot operation within the context of the World Bank-funded Urban Development Project (UDP), with the aim of launching similar operations in other city slums in the capital and elsewhere.

Under UDP Phase 1, several actions were planned and implemented in the El Mina slum under the main supervision of the implementing agency—the Urban Development Agency (ADU)—and with the support of central and local authorities and NGOs. The operation consisted of enabling long-term residents, many who had lived in the *kebbe* for more than 20 years, to move to an improved urban environment on rationalized plot patterns with registered land titles. The main components associated with upgrading the urban living environment involved the following:

- Constructing streets within the existing slum
- Upgrading the existing water supply to greatly improved service standards
- Constructing a public lighting network
- Constructing facilities, including primary and secondary schools, health centers, sanitation facilities, and cemeteries.

Freeing up rights-of-way on the proposed land, which was needed for roads and public facilities, required the removal of about 2,300 households from the El Mina slum and their relocation to a properly serviced urban area located less than a kilometer away. The urban resettlement program conducted under this project began in 2000 with the preparation of a resettlement action plan (AMEXTIPE 2000) and was successfully completed in 2004.

The integrated urban planning and participatory approach adopted for this resettlement operation was selected as an example of good practice because its successful outcomes were confirmed by independent monitoring and evaluation, it was widely disseminated on the basis of an urban resettlement guidance document, and it was eventually replicated with local funding by the government of Mauritania in other slums of the capital and in other cities.

Project Background
Project Development Context
UDP was a two-phase adaptable program loan (APL) that was approved by the World Bank's board of directors in 2001. As stated in the project appraisal document, the development and APL objectives were to support Mauritania's central and local governments in (a) improving living conditions and promoting employment opportunities in the main towns of Mauritania, especially in slums, and (b) strengthening the institutional framework and capacity for urban and land management. The International Development Association and KfW Development Bank funding obtained by the government of Mauritania in 2002 under Phase 1 of UDP amounted to US$76 million.[3] These funds were allocated to improve the quality of the urban living environment; promote economic and employment opportunities; and strengthen the institutional framework and capacity for urban and land management, management of urban environmental services, and decentralization.

UDP Phase 1 components implemented over a nine-year period between 2002 and 2011 included (a) the supply of basic municipal services in Nouakchott; (b) the supply of basic municipal services in Nouadhibou and 11 other regional capitals; (c) the servicing of urban lands in Nouakchott under the responsibility of the National Agency for Land Management; (d) the supply of water and electricity services; (e) subprojects under the "Twize" microcredit program for financing social housing and revenue generating activities; (f) institutional capacity building; and (g) project management, coordination, and monitoring.

From the beginning of project implementation in 2002, political instability in Mauritania affected the implementation of UDP. In 2003, an attempted coup undermined the constitutional stability of the country. In 2005, a second coup succeeded in breaking down constitutional order, after which the country experienced a transition period, with legislative and municipal elections following in 2006 and 2007. Just as a large group of mayors and UDP's main stakeholders and partners started to show stronger ownership for the project, another coup in 2008 disrupted the recently restored constitutional order. In 2008–09, the World Bank put disbursements related to Mauritania on hold for 15 months. A two-year extension was subsequently approved by the World Bank to complete Phase 1 activities. (See box 3.5.)

Resettlement Planning Context
Social surveys conducted for the project in 2000 (AMEXTIPE 2001) confirmed that the El Mina *kebbe* was populated by more than 40,000 of the country's poorest inhabitants, including a large proportion of members of a marginalized group known as Haratin who illegally occupied a 128-hectare extension of an industrial zone in a highly speculative and politically volatile environment (map 3.1). Most of the inhabitants had no fixed sources of income (estimated average incomes were approximately US$0.50 per day). Slum residents lived in

---

Box 3.5 Mauritania Urban Development Project at a Glance

The project development objective was to support Mauritania's central and local governments in improving living conditions and employment opportunities in the main towns of Mauritania, especially in slums, and in strengthening the institutional framework and capacity for urban and land management.

Phase 1 Components: Supply of basic municipal services in Nouakchott; supply of basic municipal services in Nouadhibou and in 11 other regional capitals; servicing of urban lands in Nouakchott under the supervision of the National Agency for Land Management; supply of water and electricity services; subprojects under the "Twize" microcredit program; institutional capacity building; and project management, coordination and monitoring

Project Implementation: 2002–11

Project Costs and Financing: US$94 million (total)—International Development Association credit of US$70 million, KfW funding of US$4 million, and counterpart financing of US$20 million by the government of Mauritania.

---

temporary dwellings made of wood and recycled materials. There were no public streets, no access to electricity or public lighting, and very limited access to drinking water and latrines. Only five public water taps were available in the slum, and water supplies were mainly provided at a high cost (US$7 per cubic meter) by itinerant vendors with donkey carts. Domestic power was provided from charcoal, kerosene, and car batteries. The clogged lanes of the slum were inaccessible to firefighting services, ambulances, public transit services, or waste collection services, and they were devoid of drainage systems. Access to public schools and health facilities was rare for residents.

Social surveys (CDHL/CP/I 2000) also revealed that 70 percent of heads of households in the El Mina slum had been living there for more than 10 years and that 35 percent had been there for 20 years or more. The average number of persons per household was 6.7 and the average number of children per household was 4.4. The proportion of women heads of households was 35 percent. About 88 percent of heads of households were illiterate or had only attended Koranic schools. Only 30 percent of male heads of households and 8 percent of female heads of households had a regular source of income. At least 25 percent of households were in need of extreme food assistance.

Thematic Analysis
Slum Upgrading and Resettlement Principles
The principles underlying the construction of a grid of public streets within the existing El Mina *kebbe* were that no household would be located more than 150 meters from a paved public street or more than 125 meters from a public drinking water tap (map 3.2). The 2,300 households (or 12,000 PAPs) that had to be relocated as a result of this effort were to be moved to a designated

Map 3.1   Nouakchott, Mauritania: Slum Areas and El Mina *Kebbe*

Note: The location of slum areas is shown in color; the El Mina *kebbe* is shown in orange.

Map 3.2 Layout of Neheza Resettlement Area for the El Mina *Kebbe*

resettlement zone known as Neheza along the western boundary of the *kebbe* on newly serviced lands that were still free of occupants.

This 48-hectare zone was considered sufficiently large to house the households to be resettled. Before the resettlement operation, it was leveled and serviced with 10 community buildings equipped with public latrines as well as with drainage systems, ditches, and cisterns. Construction of public streets and street lighting would be carried out on individual plots after the resettlement of households. Each resettled household received the following:

- Compensation for the loss of the existing housing structure on an unauthorized site, transportation costs to the resettlement site, and financial assistance toward the installation of a concrete slab and a pit for a latrine (70,000 MU or US$280)[4]
- Compensation for transition costs estimated as the equivalent of two months of a minimum salary for the head of household (30,000 MU or US$120)
- An officially recognized 120-square-meter residential plot
- Specific assistance provided to vulnerable people by the ADU's resettlement unit[5]
- Easy access to a grievance redress mechanism set up under the supervision of an independent third party—a mediator NGO recruited by the ADU.[6]

Resettled households were also provided with access to employment-generating schemes through state-funded microcredit facilities and construction-trade training programs provided by an international NGO.

Following reception of compensation payments, resettled households dismantled their makeshift shelters and reassembled them on their newly acquired plots. In addition to financial assistance toward the installation of a concrete slab and a pit for a latrine, they were provided with access to an on-site collective housing credit scheme ("Twize" program). This state-subsidized credit scheme covered 70 percent of costs toward construction of a standard one-room, 20-square-meter cement-block housing unit. Housing unit payments to be covered by homeowners were US$160 as a down payment and US$10 per month for 36 months. Many resettled households used their compensation payments to cover the down payment for construction of a new house on their plot or for construction of an additional house on their plot. As a result, the architecture of the Neheza resettlement zone is characterized by a mix of new cement-block housing units and of old reassembled shelters.

The culturally and socially adapted approach called "Twize" was developed in response to UDP's objective of poverty reduction through access to decent housing. This approach was based on collective community participation articulated with community or solidarity programs to finance and build housing "modules" (room or plot enclosure and latrine) for poor families. Twize's accomplishments in Nouakchott and Nouadhibou include the local production of 5,900 cost-controlled quality housing modules; the granting of 65,000 classic microloans destined to improve the incomes and housing of inhabitants; microloans accessible to inhabitants organized in Twize groups; the training of 1,200 professionals, including 800 in the construction sector—a priority in the project's framework; and support for the implementation of 95 urban, economic, and social microprojects. The housing scheme's success (satisfying 84 percent of targeted households) depended on the quality of the social, technical, and financial support throughout the entire process (World Bank 2013b).

Improved public street systems in the El Mina *kebbe* were accompanied by electricity distribution systems, street lighting, and improved water supply systems built along new street rights-of-way. The upgraded street systems also led to improved public transit and to the construction of community buildings (mosques) by religious groups inside the slum.

Photo 3.7 illustrates housing conditions for project-affected persons (a) before resettlement and (b) after resettlement.

Additional public investments in the El Mina slum included two new commercial market areas, including cattle and fish markets, serviced by three parking areas; five new elementary schools and three new secondary schools; and a new public health center. Public latrines were provided near community facilities and a new water tower was built in the center of the El Mina *kebbe*.

Photo 3.7 Mauritania Urban Development Project—Before and After Resettlement

a. Before resettlement

b. After resettlement

Resettlement Strategies

Public Information Program. The public information program of the El Mina resettlement operation played an important role in the success of resettlement implementation. Public information activities were adapted to the specific content of disseminated messages, with a local focus on affected households to minimize opportunistic settling in the resettlement zones and fraud during the resettlement census. Activities targeting the identification of former landowners were focused nationally.

Community representatives were recruited to serve as permanent information intermediaries in slum areas where local inhabitants initially had very little trust of outsiders. A national NGO assisted with the implementation of the public communication program during the first year of resettlement implementation. Socioeconomic baseline surveys were conducted at the beginning of the resettlement operation, particularly in the El Mina *kebbe,* to gain an understanding of the initial conditions and to support the subsequent monitoring and evaluation of post-resettlement changes (World Bank 2007a).

Institutional Framework and Local Capacity Building. The quality and stability of the institutional framework established for the resettlement operation in the El Mina slum was an important factor in ensuring the success of resettlement implementation. With the support of government authorities at the highest levels and in collaboration with community representatives, the *hakem* (prefect) and the mayor of Nouakchott had leading roles on the Resettlement and Compensation Commission (*Commission d'attribution et de compensation*) and were able to foster a durable climate of trust throughout the resettlement process. Lessons learned in the El Mina resettlement operation were subsequently applied to other slums in Nouakchott and in other cities by local authorities.

Resettlement Documentation. Documentation used for the resettlement operation in the El Mina slum proved to be highly useful. Given the extent of speculative pressures in the slum and the mobility of slum residents, particular efforts were made to properly document the identities and status of PAPs during the preparation stage, minimizing the risk of fraud during the resettlement census and ensuring that the list of PAPs would remain the same throughout the resettlement operation. Members of households being displaced were photographed during initial census surveys and officially listed in household resettlement files.

Household resettlement files produced in 2000 were maintained as official reference documents from the beginning to the end of the resettlement process. The files were systematically included in the resettlement action plan, in the official list of households to be resettled, in the eligibility criteria for resettlement and additional compensation, in the revised census data in 2003, and in the resettlement database. They were officially sealed with a bailiff to symbolically demonstrate the government's commitment to implementing the resettlement program.

Security of Land Tenure and Property Ownership. In 2003, before proceeding with resettlement implementation, ADU commissioned an updated census of households to be resettled in the El Mina slum.[7] In compliance with the Resettlement Operations Manual developed in 2003 and subsequently approved by the Resettlement and Compensation Commission, the resettlement plot attribution process was phased in at nine successive stages, with occupation of the resettlement site proceeding from north to south and freeing of rights-of-way in the El Mina *kebbe* proceeding from west to east. The attribution of plots followed the order of the resettlement census with the intent of enabling neighbors in the slum to remain neighbors at the resettlement site.

In consideration of the extreme levels of poverty experienced by El Mina slum residents, the Resettlement and Compensation Commission decided not to provide displaced households with the right to sell resettlement plots until three years after the move. Instead, in 2004, each displaced household received a numbered plastic color plot attribution badge that could not be sold. After completing formalities at ADU and receiving compensation from the bank branch set up on site by ADU, badge recipients had easy access from the resettlement plots to a housing credit office set up on site to benefit them.

Subsequently, in 2007, displaced households able to prove occupation of a resettlement plot were entitled to a payment of approximately US$40 to obtain a legal occupation permit from the government land registry (*Service des Domaines*) confirming their ownership of the residential property. This strategy sought to ensure that resettled households acquired some stability in their new living environments instead of being further marginalized by moving into other slums after accepting offers of cash for their plots.[8]

Vulnerable Persons. According to the resettlement action plan, eligible PAPs under the category of vulnerable persons included "households whose family heads were unemployed, and particularly those headed by women." Because of the large number of potentially eligible persons, eligibility criteria were revised during resettlement implementation and were restricted to "very old or physically handicapped heads of household, of either sex" (AMEXTIPE 2000). The 25 vulnerable persons identified according to these new criteria were exempted from formalities and provided with special moving assistance.

Monitoring and Evaluation. Large-scale socioeconomic household surveys were conducted by UDP before (2000) and after the resettlement program (2007 and 2012) to evaluate the extent to which resettlement outcomes in the El Mina *kebbe* were successful and livelihoods were restored after project completion. The UDP household survey on socioeconomic impacts on the Kenna El Mina area conducted in September 2007 was based on a population sample of 2,150 households selected among households resettled to the Neheza site and households that remained in the *kebbe* (World Bank 2013b). This survey was followed up by an additional UDP household survey conducted in 2012.

Results and Outcomes

According to the El Mina sourcebook (World Bank 2007a) and an independent World Bank-funded resettlement monitoring and evaluation report for El Mina (World Bank 2007b), approximately 1,400–1,500 of the resettled households participated in the subsidized housing credit system (that is, 70 percent of housing costs covered by the government) and were able to build new permanent housing structures with an almost 100 percent credit reimbursement rate over a 36-month period. Other resettled households tapped into privately held funds to build new permanent structures on their allocated plots.

Because of their limited social capital and their inability to find work, a small proportion of resettled households were never able to obtain the necessary funds to build cement-block homes on their plots. However, all of the resettled households were able to build permanent structures on their sites in one way or another. Approximately 20 vulnerable households benefited from targeted assistance by Tenmyia, an independent NGO recruited by the ADU to supervise resettlement implementation and to rebuild homes on their allocated plots.

Completion of works for infrastructure and services on the resettlement site did not proceed on pace with the relocation of displaced households—a common problem for collective resettlement programs globally. Although site leveling and laying out of roadways were completed before the allocation of replacement residential plots in 2004, public lighting was not put in place until 2005. The system of drinking water taps connected to a new water tower and reservoir in the El Mina *kebbe* was not completed until 2007. The delay was a deliberate approach of the project—the authorities were concerned about pressures by middle-income households on settlements that benefited from infrastructure improvements, given the prevailing lack of infrastructure in Nouakchott. Their approach was to deliver infrastructure gradually as they built the community, to prevent rapid gentrification (Wahba 2002).

Individual connections to the electrical distribution grid remained prohibitively expensive for most households, and in 2007, other options were under consideration. The community latrines were built at an early stage in the resettlement process and in 2007 were still in daily use, being regularly maintained by the community. Initially, individual private latrines were accepted among resettled households—with some misgivings—but they seemed to have gained greater acceptance by 2007, even as they remained difficult to maintain. In 2006–07, the markets, schools, and public health center opened as planned.

According to the 2007 socioeconomic household survey commissioned by UDP, among displaced households, 71 percent thought that housing conditions had improved; over 62 percent believed that the project had a positive impact on their access to transport; 80 percent felt that the program had helped people better organize themselves; 63 percent expressed the view that the project had increased cohesion among the population; and about 60 percent reported an improvement in contact with other parts of Nouakchott and the country at large.[9]

One of the most positive project outcomes identified by displaced households was regarding school attendance by girls—more than 70 percent of interviewed households that had relocated thought there was an improvement in this area.

Conclusions

The pilot project in the El Mina *kebbe* initiated a process of participatory and integrated development that was scaled up nationally by the government and that was gradually mainstreamed in all of the regional capitals. In El Mina, the largest and oldest of the capital's slums, socioeconomic household surveys conducted in 2007 confirmed that the social impact had been positive because slum upgrading actions had led to a relative improvement of living conditions and social cohesiveness among most inhabitants. The pilot in El Mina also had positive effects on the attendance of girls at schools, an impact felt by all of the targeted populations.

Housing conditions after the relocation of 2,300 households to the new Neheza resettlement site adjacent to El Mina were also improved. All resettled households benefited from (a) compensation for the loss of their existing housing structure on an unauthorized site, (b) transportation costs to the resettlement site, and (c) financial assistance toward the installation of a concrete slab and a pit for a latrine on their officially recognized 120-square-meter residential plot. Resettled households were also provided with compensation for transition costs and with access to employment-generating schemes through state-funded microcredit facilities and construction-trade training programs provided by an international NGO. Vulnerable persons identified among displaced households were exempted from formalities and provided with special moving assistance.

Prior to resettlement, the Neheza site was leveled and serviced with 10 community buildings equipped with public latrines as well as with drainage systems, ditches, and cisterns. Construction of public streets and street lighting was carried out on individual plots after the resettlement of households. Approximately 1,400–1,500 of the 2,300 resettled households participated in the subsidized housing credit system (Twize) and were able to build new cement-block housing structures. Other resettled households tapped into privately held funds to build new permanent structures on their allocated plots. Displaced households able to prove occupation of a resettlement plot over a period of three years were entitled to obtain a legal occupation permit from the government land registry confirming their ownership of the residential property.

The success of the El Mina pilot and its related resettlement operation affected communities in other slums that started to demand the same treatment for their slums, pushing the government to begin implementation of its large slum rehabilitation program without waiting for donor support (World Bank 2013b). The urban resettlement sourcebook produced for the UDP task team in 2004 and updated in 2007 (World Bank 2007a) was a useful reference for these operations.

Overall, UDP improved living conditions in the poor neighborhoods of Nouakchott through the application of innovative participatory and integrated development approaches. Resettlement operations conducted for displaced households in the El Mina slum dovetailed with urban renewal operations for households remaining in the slum, ensuring that everybody benefited from project activities. In addition to its quantitative benefits, the project had important qualitative and sustainable benefits with regard to social progress, with recipients reporting feeling pride about "being at home" and belonging to a nation. The project benefited from strong central and local government commitment and from the support of local communities and beneficiaries. Ultimately, it offered citizens the means to participate in important decisions taken at the local level through the development of institutional frameworks and the intervention of associations and community-based organizations. (See boxes 3.6 and 3.7.)

Box 3.6 Summary of Innovative Practices

The Urban Development Project (UDP) was particularly noteworthy for its development of an integrated urban planning approach in which resettlement operations conducted for displaced households in the El Mina slum dovetailed with urban renewal operations for the majority of households remaining in the slum. Other innovative practices included the following:

- Large-scale socioeconomic household surveys that were conducted by UDP before and after the resettlement program to evaluate the extent to which resettlement outcomes in the El Mina *kebbe* were successful and livelihoods were restored after project completion.
- The culturally and socially adapted on-site, state-subsidized, collective housing credit scheme called "Twize" was developed in response to UDP's objective of poverty reduction through access to decent housing. This approach was based on collective community participation articulated with community or solidarity programs to finance and build housing "modules" (room or plot enclosure and latrine) for poor families.
- The development of a specialized sourcebook on urban slum rehabilitation and clearance programs was subsequently used by the government of Mauritania for similar operations conducted in other slums of the capital city and other regional cities without donor support.

Box 3.7 Key Lessons Learned

- The public information program played an important role in the success of resettlement implementation. Public information activities were adapted to the specific content of disseminated messages. Community representatives were recruited to serve as permanent information intermediaries in slum areas and a national nongovernmental organization assisted with the implementation of the public communication program during the first year of resettlement implementation.

box continues next page

Box 3.7 Key Lessons Learned *(continued)*

- The quality and stability of the institutional framework established for the resettlement operation was an important factor in ensuring the success of resettlement implementation.
- The quality of documentation used for the resettlement operation proved to be critical. Given the extent of speculative pressures and the mobility of slum residents, particular efforts were made to properly document the identities and status of project-affected persons during the preparation stage.
- Successful resettlement was predicated upon an adapted strategy related to security of land tenure and property ownership to ensure that resettled households acquired some stability in their new living environments instead of being further marginalized by moving into other slums after accepting offers of cash for their plots.

Notes

1. It should be noted that over the years a number of issues have arisen related to the poor quality of construction of high rises built by private sector developers to resettle slum dwellers under the Mumbai Urban Transport Project. The rapid physical deterioration of resettlement buildings and attendant quality of life concerns for resettlers underscores the need for stringent construction supervision on similar projects in the future.

2. Drawn from World Bank and Government of Maharashtra 2009.

3. The World Bank granted an additional financing of US$25 million for the project in 2010.

4. According to a 2004 World Bank resettlement supervision report for El Mina (World Bank 2004), compensation for loss of housing was increased to 50,000 MU (US$200 in 2003) and compensation for transportation costs was increased to 20,000 MU (US$80 in 2003), enabling more resettled households to apply for subsidized housing credits under the Twize program.

5. According to the resettlement action plan (AMEXTIPE 2000), vulnerable people included disabled people, people suffering from serious illnesses, and elderly persons. Assistance to be provided included moving assistance, building assistance, and health care as needed during the moving and transition period.

6. According to the El Mina sourcebook produced for the UDP task team (World Bank 2007b), only 30 complaints were registered during the El Mina resettlement program and these were all promptly resolved.

7. According to an independent resettlement monitoring and evaluation study conducted in 2007 for the World Bank, the second census revealed that 31 households identified in the 2000 census were no longer living in the slum, while another 21 households that had been omitted in the 2000 census were registered as households to be resettled. Another 40–50 households settled in the area after the resettlement cut-off date and were considered ineligible for compensation and relocation to the resettlement site. However, the ADU gave these households assistance in finding other living sites in the El Mina slum.

8. According to the resettlement action plan (AMEXTIPE 2000), although land attribution policy in Nouakchott is guided by social principles, with land occupation permits

as cheap as US$0.25 per square meter, land speculation is taking place on a large scale on the outskirts of the city. The poorest people tend to sell the land occupation permits awarded to them by the government and remain squatting in *kebbes* and *gazras*, a practice that is widely tolerated. By law, land that remains unoccupied and undeveloped is supposed to revert to the public domain, but this is not enforced and much titled land remains devoid of either occupation or development.

9. Drawn from the summary of UDP's household survey on socioeconomic impacts on the Kenna El Mina area in September 2007 (World Bank 2013b).

References

AMEXTIPE. 2000. "Programme de Développement Urbain, Restructuration du quartier El Mina à Nouakchott." Plan d'Action de Réinstallation, préparé par F. Giovannetti, AMEXTIPE.

———. 2001. "Programme d'A mélioration des Conditions de vie dans les Quartiers Périphériques et Spontanés de Nouakchott." Étude d'impact social El Mina, Riyad, Dar Naim, Teyarett-Nord, préparée par A. Martella, (Version préliminaire, Janvier), AMEXTIPE.

CDHL/CP/I (Commissariat aux Droits de l'Homme, à la Lutte contre la Pauvreté et à l'Insertion). 2000. "Urbaplan." Rapport 3 pour le Commissariat aux Droits de l'Homme, à la Lutte Contre la Pauvreté et à l'Insertion, cited in A. Martella, 2001, CDHL/CP/I.

MMRDA (Mumbai Metropolitan Region Development Authority). 2002. "Mumbai Urban Transport Project (MUTP)." Resettlement Action Plan, Revised Final Report (April), MMRDA, Mumbai.

TISS (Tata Institute of Social Sciences). 2008. "Impact Assessment of Resettlement Implementation under Mumbai Urban Transport Project (MUTP)." Prepared for the Mumbai Metropolitan Region Development Authority (March), TISS, Mumbai. http://www-wds.worldbank.org/external/default/WDSContentServer/WDSP/IB/20 12/08/16/000386194_20120816030102/Rendered/PDF/SR420P050668000080902 0120Box370092B.pdf.

Wahba, Sameh Naguib. 2002. "From Land Distribution to Integrated Development: The Evolution and Impact of Shelter and Poverty Alleviation Policies in Marginalized Settlements in Nouakchott, Mauritania." PhD thesis. Harvard University, Cambridge, MA.

World Bank. 2004. "Suivi de l'opération El-Mina—Impact social." Resettlement Supervision Report for El Minaprepared for the Urban Development Project Task Team, World Bank, Washington, DC.

———. 2007a. "L'opération de réinstallation des ménages déplacés par la restructuration du quartier précaire d'El Mina à Nouakchott—Sourcebook—Opération 2000–2007." El-Mina Resettlement Operation Sourcebook, produced for the Urban Development Project Task Team, World Bank, Washington, DC.

———. 2007b. "Annexe 3—Mise en œuvre de la réinstallation à la Kebbe d'El Mina, Version provisoire." Independent Resettlement Monitoring and Evaluation Study, carried out for the Urban Development Project Task Team, World Bank, Washington, DC.

———. 2011. *Mumbai Urban Transport Project (MUTP)*. Implementation Completion Report. Washington, DC: World Bank.

———. 2013a. "Mumbai Urban Transport Project (MUTP): Sixth and Final Progress Report on Implementation of the Management Action Plan in Response to the

Inspection Panel's Report and Recommendations." Final Management Response to the Inspection Panel, World Bank, Washington, DC.

———. 2013b. *UDP Implementation Completion and Results Report*. Washington, DC: World Bank.

World Bank and Government of Maharashtra. 2009. *India—Mumbai Urban Transport Project: Guidance Note on Urban Resettlement*. Washington, DC: World Bank.

World Bank and Ministry of Finance of India. 2012. "Urban Resettlement, Mumbai Urban Transport Project." Innovation Note No. 7, with contributions from Satya N. Mishra and S.V.R. Srinivas. World Bank, Washington, DC.

CHAPTER 4

Livelihood Restoration for Informal Urban Occupations: Examples from Morocco and Pakistan

Artisan and Fez Medina Project in Morocco

Rationale for Case Study Selection

With a population of about 1 million, the imperial city of Fez is the third largest urban area in Morocco. It is the capital of traditional Moroccan culture and is renowned as a historic place of learning, an Islamic pilgrimage destination, and a center for traditional artisanal arts.

The site of the Artisan and Fez Medina Project is located in Fès el Bali (or old Fez), the larger of the two historic medinas[1] of Fez. The medina is listed as a United Nations Educational, Scientific, and Cultural Organization (UNESCO) World Heritage Site. With a population estimated at 150,000, it constitutes a dense and intricate maze of open and covered streets, winding paths, and intimate squares built according to the medieval Islamic urban settlement pattern. It is considered one of the largest car-free urban areas in the world. The ninth-century Karaouiyine mosque in the medina is among the most famous in the Islamic world. It houses a university that is thought to be the world's oldest. The medina attracts about 170,000 tourists annually—about 10 percent of all foreign visitors to Morocco (World Bank, n.d.).

The Artisan and Fez Medina Project proposed to redevelop a small neighborhood abutting a square at one of the main entrances to Fès el Bali and to restore four historic *foundouks* (commercial hostels) along the well-trodden tourist trails to enhance local cultural and tourism attractions and sustain local handicraft industries. The square, known as Place Lalla Ydouna (PLY), is located close to the Karaouiyine mosque and is renowned as a historical center for artisanal copperware products—such as lamps and teapots—and as the nexus of a complex artisanal production chain.

This case highlights an innovative urban resettlement approach adopted to ensure the transfer of a complex artisanal production chain from the Fez Medina to the Ain Nokbi industrial park located close to the medina. The overarching goals of the approach were to do the following:

- Maintain livelihoods of copperware artisans and employees during the transition period and improve livelihoods after the transition through upgraded production facilities and an enhanced working environment.
- Ensure that owners and employees of other relocated artisanal production facilities and businesses received full support in the restoration of their livelihoods.
- Provide improved housing conditions to relocated residential households.
- Focus on the needs of the most vulnerable artisanal employees (the elderly, women, apprentices ages 15–18, and children under age 15 years).
- Support the daily on-site presence of a local social nongovernmental organization (NGO) and make use of a credible grievance mechanism to resolve issues during resettlement implementation.
- Provide flexible, adaptive, and well-funded management of resettlement implementation in a complex historical urban environment.

Project Background
Resettlement Planning Context

Funding for the Artisan and Fez Medina Project was provided by the Millennium Challenge Corporation (MCC), a U.S. government development agency, from 2009 to 2013. Consistent with MCC's environmental and social requirements, resettlement was planned and implemented in compliance with the World Bank's Operational Policy on Involuntary Resettlement (OP 4.12). The project was jointly developed with the government of Morocco as part of a five-year compact signed between the United States and Moroccan governments and was implemented in collaboration with UNESCO. It built on the World Bank–funded Morocco Cultural Heritage Project, which was implemented in the Fez Medina during the 1990s. Funding for the resettlement component of the project was jointly covered by the MCC for compensation and livelihood restoration costs related to informal artisanal activities and by the government of Morocco for all property acquisitions related to expropriation of PLY and two other foundouks to be restored.

The institutional framework for resettlement rested on two Moroccan government agencies: the Agence de Partenariat pour le Progrès (APP), which reported directly to the prime minister in Rabat, and a project management unit (UGP or unité de gestion de projet) set up in Fez under the Agence de Dédensification et de Réhabilitation de Fès (ADER-Fès), an urban renewal agency that had been previously created with the support of the World Bank. The resettlement planning and implementation process was supported by national, regional, and local authorities and by local artisan associations that played a large role in resettlement planning and implementation.

This process was conducted notably through a regional steering committee (*comité de pilotage*) set up under the authority of the *wali* (governor) of the Fès-Boulmane region and a local grievance committee (*comité de proximité*) established by order of the wali in June 2011 to handle local grievances during resettlement implementation.

The center of artisanal copperware production (*dinanderie*)—for example, door ornaments, decorative lamps, platters, and teapots—in the Fez Medina was located in PLY. The neighborhood was divided in half by a small urban river (Oued El Jawahir), forming an intricate network of dinandier producers, specialized and nonspecialized subcontractors, suppliers, and retailers as well as a number of related artisanal and commercial activities such as warehouses, tanneries, leather processing workshops, traditional trimming makers (*passementiers*) and slipper producers and vendors (*babouchiers*). This network was loosely connected to surrounding neighborhoods through a web of commercial relationships and was supported by a variety of specialized and nonspecialized workers and apprentices whose numbers fluctuated according to the type, volume, and number of orders and depending on the time of year.

One of the driving forces behind the relocation of artisanal copperware production activities from the medina was the incompatibility with neighboring residential uses. Copperware production workshops were tiny, unsafe, and poorly adapted to industrial processes. A number of copperware production workshops used polluting industrial processes such as electrolysis. The policies of the Urban Commune of Fez required that the artisanal copperware production chain be relocated to a more appropriate industrial environment in the neighboring Ain Nokbi industrial park that had been established for such purposes. Earlier efforts to resettle artisanal copperware producers to Ain Nokbi undertaken in 2000–2005 by the commune had been largely unsuccessful, and only a few producers had relocated their units before the start-up process of the Fez Medina resettlement. Those who had moved complained of being disconnected from the production chain and of being relocated to a largely empty and unsafe work environment.

Other reasons behind the relocation of artisanal copperware production to the Ain Nokbi industrial park included the need (1) to provide artisans with the necessary facilities and working conditions to enable them to upgrade the quality of their products in an increasingly competitive international market and (2) to encourage young male and female apprentices to pursue traditional artisanal activities because the workforce was aging and becoming less capable of adjusting to new market conditions.

Scope of Resettlement

A key goal of the Artisan and Fez Medina Project was to attract tourists and highlight copperware handicrafts through new construction and restoration of historic buildings in PLY as well as through restoration of four historic foundouks in the vicinity of PLY. Map 4.1 illustrates the proposed interventions in PLY. Shaded buildings in pale grey were considered of lesser architectural value and

Map 4.1 Layout of Proposed Works in the Place Lalla Ydouna Neighborhood of the Fez Medina

were to be demolished after completion of the resettlement program. A number of artisanal workshops and showrooms, restaurants and cafes, and a small boutique hotel were to be built in their place around redesigned public spaces created on either side of a reprofiled section of the Oued Al Jawahir.[2] In agreement with UNESCO, buildings shaded in dark grey were considered to be of a higher architectural and heritage value and were to be restored after the completion of the resettlement program. Buildings highlighted in yellow had yet to be evacuated at the time the map was produced.

The project required moving a total of 194 informal sector "polluting" and "nonpolluting" artisanal and commercial activities from PLY to a neighboring artisanal industrial park at Ain Nokbi without disrupting artisanal activities and without affecting the historic character of one of the medina's main entrances. This move was accomplished by constructing 22 new production units for 26 PLY copperware producers and a new artisanal production center (foundouk) for 77 PLY copperware subcontractors at Ain Nokbi (See photos 4.1a and b).

A few other artisanal activities in PLY—a tannery, a metal workshop, two leather processing workshops, and 11 trimming makers—were considered to be too polluting or too noisy to remain after the site's rehabilitation; they were designated for permanent relocation. Another 16 vacant commercial spaces and

Photo 4.1 Artisan and Fez Medina Project, Morocco: Before and After Resettlement

a. Before resettlement

b. After resettlement

storehouses were also designated for permanent relocation. A total of 47 "non-polluting" artisanal and commercial activities at PLY were considered appropriate for returning to PLY after project completion and therefore were designated for temporary relocation while work was conducted at PLY. Few artisans or workers at PLY lived on site; most commuted from within or outside the medina. Only eight households in PLY were required to relocate because of the project.

Resettlement activities required in the four foundouks included the permanent relocation of 21 warehouses and empty spaces from Foundouk Staounyyine and the temporary relocation of 11 artisanal workshops and businesses for the duration of its restoration. Resettlement activities required for the other foundouks (Barka and the adjacent foundouks Chemaine-Sbitryyine) were limited to the temporary in situ relocation of 13 artisanal workshops and businesses during the renovations (*opérations-tiroirs*).

Ultimately, a total of 1,044 project-affected persons (PAPs) were identified in the context of the Fez Medina resettlement action plan (RAP). Households to be relocated from PLY included two owners and six tenants. Artisanal and commercial activities employed 682 mostly part-time informal employees, including specialized workers, apprentices, and helpers. Many artisans and most employees to be relocated were very poor. Most employees were males between the ages of 18 and 59 (549), but a number of them were female (98), elderly (21 men and 3 women 60 years or older), underage (35 employees between the ages of 15 and 18, including 3 females), or illegally employed children (4 employees ages 15 or younger, including 1 female). The 45 other artisanal workshops, businesses, and warehouses that had to be relocated from the four foundouks employed another 24 employees, who were 23 men and 1 woman 18–59 years of age.

Thematic Analysis
Preparation of Resettlement Action Plan

Resettlement activities were planned over two years, from July 2009 to July 2011, on the basis of in-depth socioeconomic surveys and asset inventories carried out in five historic sites in the medina: PLY—located at one of the main entrances to the medina—and foundouks Barka, Chemaine-Sbitryyine, and Staounyyine—strategically located along tourist routes in the medina. Because of the limited time frame of the compact, only two years remained after completion of the RAP for resettlement implementation, including construction of replacement workshops at Ain Nokbi and subsequent demolition work and construction and restoration work at PLY and in the foundouks.

Conducting the socioeconomic surveys required the full support of local artisan associations that explained the purpose and modalities of the surveys to initially reticent workshop owners (*maalems*). The artisan associations also assisted surveyors throughout the process. Artisans had limited trust in the authorities, particularly in the aftermath of the unsuccessful resettlement program previously conducted by the Urban Commune of Fez, and they were uneasy about surveyors asking questions of their employees. The census of PAPs and related socioeconomic surveys served as the basis for establishing a resettlement database of eligible artisans, businesses, and households.

A particular focus of the socioeconomic surveys was determining the footprint of the resettlement operation. There were concerns that the economic impact of relocating part of the artisanal copperware production chain from PLY to Ain Nokbi could extend deep into the medina, disrupting long-term business relationships and intricate social networks. The design of the surveys enabled the study team to confirm that commercial relationships with other artisanal producers outside PLY were sporadic or occasional and that the economic and social footprint of the resettlement operation was mostly limited to the project area.

The socioeconomic surveys and focus groups carried out with artisans and their employees also enabled the social team responsible for the RAP to determine the various categories of commercial activities at PLY and in the foundouks; to gain an understanding of their economic and social interrelations, strengths, and vulnerabilities; and to find agreement with the artisanal associations on levels of compensation and assistance required for each eligible category of activity being relocated under the program. The principles for each category of eligibility were agreed to jointly, and they subsequently served as a foundation for public information meetings held with PAPs and for the deliberations of the local grievance committee set up to review claims or complaints that emerged during implementation.

Resettlement Strategies

The development of specific resettlement strategies in collaboration with the local associations of artisans constituted a critical—and time consuming—component of the RAP preparation. It involved both the establishment of agreed-on compensation and assistance principles for each category of PAP and agreed-on relocation strategies, taking into account time constraints and the need to move all elements of the production chain within a short time.

Compensation and Assistance Principles. A major element in establishing agreed-on compensation and assistance principles was getting local artisans to understand that the application of the World Bank's policy on involuntary resettlement meant that compensation would be applied to informal sector activities on the basis of agreed-on, fair, and equitable principles that applied to all. In the local Moroccan expropriation context, informal commercial activities had no official value and therefore were ineligible for compensation. As a result, such activities were subject to case-by-case negotiations during which the informal artisans were at a clear disadvantage. Once the applicable principles of OP 4.12 were fully understood by artisans and government agencies, a detailed entitlement matrix was developed and agreed to by all parties for each category of PAP. This matrix included the following complex cases:

- Artisanal workshops that were temporarily closed or used as temporary warehouses because of slowdowns in business

- Unregistered squatters and undocumented residents who had occupied the square for a long time but were not recognized by the authorities
- Owners of artisanal production units at Ain Nokbi who had moved under the previous resettlement program and who felt that they should be compensated for the costs they had incurred in building their own workshops
- Underage children working illegally in the workshops as children of the owners or because they had no other place to go
- Women who were working without any rights as replacements for child employees who had recently been barred by law from employment in artisanal workshops
- Elderly persons (ages 60 years or older) working in difficult conditions in artisanal workshops who hoped to retire when they had enough money
- Workers who feared that their compensation would be seized by the state because they owed back taxes.

Given the levels of uncertainty involved in defining the resettlement budget in a complex urban environment, the contingencies defined in the RAP for compensation and livelihood restoration related to artisanal and commercial activities were set at 35 percent, and the contingencies for the cost of relocating residential households were established at 50 percent.

Resettlement Measures. The resettlement strategy adopted for the artisanal copperware production chain comprised three core elements:

- Joint planning of individual and collective production units in the Ain Nokbi industrial park outside the medina and related facilities and services with the local associations of artisans (for example, dedicated bus service, commercial amenities, police, and public health services)
- Construction of a new location for the Association of Copperware Artisans to use as a place to showcase their wares and as an artisanal training center
- Temporary relocation of artisanal producers and subcontractors to two other foundouks in the industrial park to allow for lengthier construction times for individual and collective replacement units at Ain Nokbi.

Construction of the individual and collective replacement production units in the Ain Nokbi industrial park and of a new location for the Association of Copperware Artisans was funded by the MCC under the Artisan and Fez Medina Project. The Fès-Boulemane region and the Urban Commune of Fez covered the building costs of the two foundouks to be used temporarily for the relocation of PLY producers and subcontractors with the intent of using these two buildings for the relocation of other artisanal producers and subcontractors from the medina at a later time. The Urban Commune of Fez funded the dedicated bus service, commercial amenities, police, and public health services, as well as other services that were required at Ain Nokbi to ensure the viability of the site as a work environment for women and men.

Given the compact's brief timeline, it was impossible to guarantee the return of 47 "nonpolluting" artisanal and commercial units to PLY considered suitable for resettlement in the project site after work was completed. Consequently, a US$1 million contingency fund was set aside in the RAP to compensate owners of these units for long-term commercial rent (*pas de porte*) in case they had to find replacement premises of equivalent value in the medina. In this event, they would also be guaranteed priority access to the redeveloped square following project completion.

Security of Land Tenure and Property Ownership. Individual and collective production units built and serviced for resettled artisanal producers and subcontractors in the Ain Nokbi industrial park and in the new location for the Association of Copperware Artisans were transferred to the beneficiaries with full title, and related titling and registration costs were assumed by the project. The 77 subcontractors relocated to the MCC-funded foundouk at Ain Nokbi were also to acquire title to their specific units inside the foundouk and were to be provided with technical assistance to manage the building as a collective unit.[3]

Vulnerable Persons. Specific assistance measures were put into place for the most vulnerable PAP employees (the elderly, women, young apprentices, and underage children). They included the following:

- Funding the return to school of four underage child employees
- Functional literacy and vocational training programs for vulnerable PAPs through negotiation of an agreement with an artisanal training center in Fez to provide vocational training programs to eligible vulnerable PAPs (20 young female employees and 35 young apprentices) and to provide specially tailored functional literacy programs to 75 ineligible older female employees in collaboration with their employers
- Payment of additional compensation for temporary loss of income to 21 men and 3 women ages 60 or older given their greater difficulty in adjusting to new work environments
- Financial assistance for increased transportation costs to all PAP employees based on the value of a two-year public transit bus pass.

Grievance Redress Mechanisms. A local grievance committee was set up by order of the Fès-Boulmane regional governor in June 2011. The committee comprised representatives of UGP/ADER-Fès, local authorities, and local artisan associations. As required, it met throughout the two-year resettlement implementation process, and proceedings were made public by UGP/ADER-Fès. The committee successfully processed a number of cases during resettlement implementation.

Monitoring and Evaluation. The social unit of UGP/ADER-Fès, with the assistance of a locally recruited social NGO, completed a number of field surveys to document post-resettlement conditions for several categories of PAPs. Given limited resources and time constraints, these efforts mainly focused on the following:

- The eight residential households relocated from PLY
- The 47 "nonpolluting" artisanal workshops and businesses that had to leave PLY on the basis of payment of their "pas de portes"
- The four PAP employees ages 15 years or younger assisted in returning to school
- The 98 female PAP employees and 35 underage PAP employees assisted in registering in functional literacy programs or technical training programs provided through the Centre Batha-Fès or through other registered training centers.

Resettlement Implementation

Management of Resettlement Implementation. Updating of the census of artisanal workshop and business employees at PLY and in the four foundouks was conducted in the spring of 2012. The 2010 census of employees was considered outdated because of the high turnover rate in artisanal workshops.

Payments of compensation packages to owners of artisanal workshops and businesses and to residential households were completed as planned by mid-2012, before the clearance of all occupants from PLY and the foundouks. Both payments by the government of Morocco for land acquisition under the national expropriation law and payments funded by MCC for the loss of informal sector activities, in compliance with the World Bank's Involuntary Resettlement Policy, were completed as planned. However, large numbers of small compensation payments to the employees of resettled artisanal workshops and businesses by central authorities at APP were delayed and were completed only after their relocation from PLY and the foundouks.

Compensation payments for long-term commercial rents, moving costs, and lost incomes were made to 15 "polluting" artisans and 13 temporarily closed businesses for leaving PLY. Payments were also made to 47 "nonpolluting" artisans and business owners who would probably not be able to return to PLY after the construction and restoration work was completed, with the caveat that those artisans and business owners would have to apply the compensation to the acquisition of replacement long-term commercial rents in the medina. The same conditions were set for 30 artisans and business owners from Foundouk Staounyyine who would probably not be able to return to the foundouk after the restoration work was completed. UGP/ADER-Fès followed up with these artisans and business owners to ensure that they had all rented new artisanal or commercial sites after receiving their compensation.

Implementation Challenges. Unplanned construction delays for individual and collective replacement units in the Ain Nokbi industrial park combined with production constraints for artisanal copperware producers necessitated that additional compensation be paid to producers and subcontractors for lost income during the mid-2012 to mid-2013 transition period. The public bus company in

Fez went out of business, and the new private bus service refused to honor agreements made with PAPs, requiring the resettlement implementation unit to find alternative solutions in collaboration with artisanal workers. Negotiations with appropriate training centers also took a long time and caused unpredicted delays.

Unforeseen permanent and temporary resettlement in and around the square and in the vicinity of the historic foundouks that were to be restored also required that additional compensation payments be made to new PAPs. Twenty-five artisanal workshops and businesses had to be permanently or temporarily relocated from the foundouks or from their immediate vicinity for safety reasons. These activities employed an additional 11 people. Three additional residential households had to be temporarily relocated from the vicinity of the foundouks, including two that required an additional year of rent at an alternative location to cover the duration of the renovations.

Additional compensation was required for nine cases at PLY that were submitted for review to the local grievance committee and that resulted in some favorable decisions, including claims submitted by the Coopérative des Tanneurs, whose workshops were inaccessible during the RAP census surveys.

Such unexpected events put pressure on the resettlement implementation team and required that previous agreements with groups of PAPs be renegotiated under difficult circumstances and that additional rounds of compensation payments be programmed and implemented on their behalf. These events also necessitated that additional resettlement surveys and negotiations be conducted with newly identified PAPs at the same time that monitoring and evaluation of the ongoing resettlement activities was being rolled out.

Local Capacity Building for Resettlement

At the onset of the project, local municipal capacity for managing complex urban resettlement programs was relatively limited. The institutional framework for resettlement rested on two Moroccan government agencies that had little to no experience with resettlement—APP, which reported directly to the prime minister in Rabat, and a UGP set up in Fez under ADER-Fès, an urban renewal agency that had been established with the support of the World Bank. Earlier efforts by the Urban Commune of Fez in 2000–2005 to resettle artisanal copperware producers to Ain Nokbi had been largely unsuccessful. Only a few producers had relocated their units before the start-up process of the Fez Medina resettlement. Previous resettlement activities conducted by ADER-Fès in the context of other urban renewal programs in the medina had also met with limited success and had left a legacy of distrust among local artisans.

Preparation and implementation of the project RAP was conducted over a four-year period in close collaboration with local authorities and local artisan associations, requiring significant capacity building efforts on the part of the partner agencies involved in training, public awareness activities, and specialized technical assistance. This goal was achieved by MCC and APP through the deployment of specialized supervision and oversight resources throughout the planning and implementation process. MCC and APP planned oversight missions with international resettlement specialists every trimester throughout the planning process and even more frequently during the two-year implementation process. This planning enabled local municipal agencies and concerned populations to gain a better understanding of resettlement processes conducted according to international standards and to compare obtained results with previously unsuccessful resettlement efforts.

Results and Outcomes

Field surveys conducted to document post-resettlement conditions confirmed that the eight residential households relocated from PLY were successfully resettled inside and outside the medina. The 47 "nonpolluting" artisanal workshops and businesses that had to leave PLY on the basis of payment of their "pas de portes" were able to reestablish themselves at other locations in the medina. All affected underage child employees successfully returned to school. Financial assistance for functional literacy programs or technical training programs provided through the Centre Batha-Fès or other registered training centers for 98 female PAP employees and for 35 underage PAP employees (ages 15–18 years) proved highly successful, with a 100 percent participation rate. Vocational training programs and functional literacy programs enabled a number of female employees to opt for new career paths.

The permanent relocation of copperware artisans from PLY to modern individual and collective production units in the Ain Nokbi industrial park outside the medina and the provision of related facilities and services have enabled the full restoration of the production chain. Construction of a new locale for the Association of Copperware Artisans at Ain Nokbi offered the artisans a showcase for their wares. An artisanal training center used for functional literacy programs provided by the Batha-Fès Artisanal Training Center was designated for female PAP employees. Eight copperware producers from PLY benefited from the reimbursement for the production units already built or in the process of being built at Ain Nokbi as well as for related moving costs and lost income.

Full ownership of individual workshops in the newly built subcontractor foundouk at Ain Nokbi and the establishment of a functional association have provided greater security to subcontractors in the copperware production chain. The subcontractor foundouk includes facilities specifically designated for women as well as a day care center for the children of female employees.

Additional commitments made by the project steering committee in the first half of 2012 to upgrade the quality of public services available at Ain Nokbi were also largely met. These included the provision by the Région de Fès-Boulmane and the Urban Commune of Fez for a dedicated public bus route to Ain Nokbi, as well as regular police patrols, weekly visits by medical personnel, improved street lighting, and the right to operate a few food stalls at Ain Nokbi, thereby largely addressing the health and safety concerns raised by artisans during the preparation of the RAP.

Priority access to artisanal shops in the redeveloped square and restored commercial buildings still await project completion, which is being pursued under government of Morocco funding.

Conclusions

The Artisan and Fez Medina Project now serves as a model for future urban resettlement operations in the city of Fez. Although high urban resettlement costs are of concern to local and national authorities, the fact that the resettlement program conducted for the project was carried out in full collaboration with the beneficiaries constitutes a notable accomplishment in the context of the Arab Spring. Resettlement procedures and public consultation processes adopted for the project have since been applied by the implementation agency ADER-Fès to other resettlement activities in the Fez Medina. See boxes 4.1 and 4.2.

Box 4.1 Summary of Innovative Practices

Joint funding of the resettlement by the Millennium Challenge Corporation and the government of Morocco constituted an innovative approach that built on the respective strengths of Moroccan expropriation procedures. Such procedures are well adapted to the compensation of formally registered land and property assets and to the World Bank's Operational Policy on Involuntary Resettlement (OP 4.12), which is better adapted to the management of losses related to informal sector activities. Other innovative practices included the following:

- Planning and implementing the resettlement census and socioeconomic studies in close collaboration with the local artisan associations
- Defining the eligibility requirements for each category of project-affected persons (PAPs) in the resettlement action plan's entitlement matrix in close collaboration with all concerned parties
- Designing the resettlement strategy, including construction of temporary work units, in collaboration with members of the artisanal production chain
- Negotiating an agreement with an artisanal training center in Fez to provide vocational training programs to eligible vulnerable PAPs (20 young female employees and 35 young apprentices) and to provide specially tailored functional literacy programs to 75 ineligible older female employees in collaboration with their employers.

Box 4.2 Key Lessons Learned

- The complexity of relocating an artisanal production chain in a historical urban setting was compounded by external factors such as construction delays for replacement units, overall project delays, and unforeseen additional resettlement and compensation. Some of these problems were related to the specific challenges associated with working in a historic medina, where resettlement surveys can be particularly prone to errors and where buildings are often at risk of structural failure during demolition and restoration work.
- The management of unplanned events required large resettlement contingency funds and substantial investments in the supervision of the resettlement implementation. Going

box continues next page

Box 4.2 Key Lessons Learned (*continued*)

forward, planners of similar urban resettlement operations should emphasize adaptability and flexibility in resettlement plans, including providing for important contingencies in resettlement budgets and additional supervision resources during resettlement implementation.

- The successful resettlement of an artisanal copperware production chain from the medina was largely due to (1) the daily on-site presence of the social unit of the project management unit and Agence de Dédensification et de Réhabilitation de Fès and the local social nongovernmental organization recruited for these purposes; (2) the credibility achieved by the local grievance committee; (3) the availability of substantial contingency funds to cover unforeseen construction delays and additional resettlement requirements; and (4) the supervision and oversight resources that the Millennium Challenge Corporation and Agence de Partenariat pour le Progrès deployed throughout the planning and implementation process.

Sustainable Development of the Walled City of Lahore Project, Pakistan

Rationale for Case Study Selection

Lahore is one of the oldest living cities in Pakistan, documented by historians and geographers since 1021 AD. During the Mughal period (1524–1707), Lahore experienced unprecedented development, becoming a center of architectural, cultural, and economic activities. Over time, however, the historic core of the city—the Walled City of Lahore—has been neglected, evidenced by a progressive population decline, the pauperization of residential areas in favor of rapidly expanding commercial districts, the rapid demolition or erosion of heritage assets by commercial interests, poor maintenance of infrastructure, and a resulting decline in the quality of life. This neglect has kept the vast tourism potential of the Walled City of Lahore (WCL) unrealized.

There has been a growing and widely shared acknowledgment that Pakistan's cultural heritage assets are rich in potential for contributing to the reduction of poverty and for triggering economic activity if they can be appropriately tapped for cultural tourism. This, in turn, could contribute toward a softer impression of Pakistan.

In 2006, recognizing the need to preserve and restore the cultural heritage of the historic city and to promote tourism and adaptive reuse, the government of Punjab, in partnership with the World Bank, launched a pilot project called the Sustainable Development of Walled City Lahore Project (SDWCLP). Its objectives were urban regeneration and restoration of the historic core of Lahore. The initiative was a component within a larger effort supporting performance-based management—the Punjab Municipal Services Improvement Project.

This case study highlights SDWCLP's innovative urban involuntary resettlement approach, which took special care to assist the resettlement of informal shopkeepers and their employees, as well as households and residents in the project area of the WCL. Livelihoods were sustained and community-level service delivery was improved.

The most significant factor in the success of SDWCLP's urban involuntary resettlement was the development and implementation of a robust RAP that included a highly successful model of social mobilization; benefit-sharing through a livelihoods lens; citizen-led regeneration; and a consistent and field-based monitoring and oversight strategy. The lessons learned confirm that this type of approach can bring about positive and sustainable urban involuntary resettlement outcomes. This type of approach also demonstrates the importance of incorporating resettlement as an integrated method of urban regeneration.

Project Background
Cultural Heritage
There is an old Pakistani saying, "A person who has not seen Lahore is not born" (Ebbe 1998, 14). Many Pakistanis consider WCL to be the cultural heart of the country. The walled city flourished as a regional center under the Mughals in the seventeenth and eighteenth centuries, but fell into decline in the mid-nineteenth century when it came under British control. The colonial masters shifted their attention to the newly established cantonment for the garrison and estates of civil service officers. Today, Lahore is the administrative capital of Punjab and an important industrial and commercial center.

WCL, located in the northwestern corner of Lahore, contains an astonishing array of historic cultural assets, including mosques, forts, gateways, residential buildings, palaces, tombs, alleyways, and open squares. In addition to this rich architectural heritage, an intangible heritage thrives in the form of traditional cultural activities, economic initiatives, and social relationships. However, WCL is also currently home to some of the poorest people working in metropolitan Lahore. Results from a baseline socioeconomic household survey showed a gross monthly income of Prs 16,222 (US$165) for an average family of 5.7 persons. Moreover, about 5–17 percent of WCL's population falls in the lowest-income quintile. Crime levels are high and literacy rates low. For many of these WCL inhabitants—crammed into 4 square kilometers and making up a fraction of Lahore's 7 million residents—quality municipal services are rare.

Sustainable Development
Just before the World Bank Board of Directors approved the Punjab Municipal Services Improvement Project, the government of Punjab requested that World Bank management provide funding for a cultural heritage project. Because cultural heritage work in Pakistan had experienced a long hiatus, it was agreed that a cultural heritage component should be added to the Punjab Municipal Services Improvement Project to enable the undertaking of the complex preparatory work needed for such an initiative. The SDWCLP pilot would include preparatory activities and the piloting of methods for a full-fledged cultural heritage project in the future.

The Shahi Guzargah (Royal Trail) and the streets emanating from it were selected as the pilot for implementation to showcase methods and benefits of the conservation of cultural assets and their productive use and reuse. The Royal Trail was the route taken by the Mughal emperors to reach the royal fort palace when they were returning from Delhi to Lahore. They entered WCL through the Delhi Gate, bathed in the Shahi Hammam (Royal Bath), and prayed in the Wazir Khan Mosque on the way to the fort. Over the years, many of the private buildings along the route had fallen into disrepair, had been replaced, or had the adjacent public spaces encroached on.

Neighborhoods along the Royal Trail—and the infrastructure serving them—were in serious peril. Overcrowding, inappropriate zoning, pollution, and decay threatened the historic fabric of the area. In 1947, with the birth of Pakistan, there was a mass exodus of Hindus and Sikhs from WCL, and an even greater influx of refugees from across the Indian border. Because of the desperate need for shelter, property that had been vacated by earlier residents was occupied by refugees. Historic houses, many stories tall as generations of families built on top of each other, remained neglected as multiple families occupied them. Moreover, occupants began to encroach on public space, dictated by their need for more room. This encroachment was compounded by municipal negligence in service delivery, creating slum-like conditions that had major negative sociocultural and economic impacts on the approximately 150,000 residents of WCL.

SDWCLP aimed to reduce poverty and initiate economic activity in WCL; to improve the quality and standard of living for the residents; to improve the municipal services; to restore, conserve, and put into adaptive use cultural heritage assets; and to enhance local ownership of the cultural heritage (box 4.3).

Box 4.3 Punjab Municipal Services Improvement Project at a Glance

The project development objective was to improve the viability and effectiveness of the urban services provided by the participating Tehsil Municipal Administrations (TMAs) and to make such investments sustainable and replicable in other TMAs through the creation of a performance-based management framework at both the TMA and provincial levels.

Component 1—Support for TMAs through Capacity and Development Grants: Capacity grants were used to support institutional development through improvements in urban planning (geographic information system–based land use and infrastructure mapping), financial management, investment planning for service delivery, operation and maintenance of assets, computerized complaint tracking and resolution, and customer surveys to monitor the performance of TMAs. Development grants were used to finance infrastructure investments (subprojects) in the TMAs, and were to be awarded on the basis of performance.

Component 2—Support for Other Institutions through Capacity Building and Other Activities: This component supported capacity building of the Planning and Development Department, including the newly established Sustainable Development of the Walled City of Lahore unit responsible for implementation of the Cultural Heritage initiative, and the Local Government and Rural Development Department, including the Punjab Municipal Development Fund Company.

Cost of Project: US$59 million.

Project Implementation: 2006–13.

Source: World Bank 2006.

A particular focus was on nurturing cultural tourism with the development of restaurants, hotels, tourist transportation, and handicrafts. Most important, the community would be involved in the development process.

SDWCLP focused on undertaking studies to recommend a rationalization for institutional mandates regarding the management of heritage assets; propose appropriate amendments to existing legislative frameworks; and implement a pilot project that included the creation of a heritage trail to showcase methods and the benefits of the conservation of cultural assets and their productive use or reuse.[4]

The pilot project included (a) the provision of new municipal infrastructure and services (below ground as far as possible), including electrical, communication, water supply, storm drainage, sewerage, and gas supply networks that were obsolete, inadequate, or completely absent, and (b) the rehabilitation of the urban fabric through facade and street improvements. (See map 4.2 and photos 4.2a and b.)

To begin work on the conservation, rehabilitation, and infrastructure improvement, various preparatory activities were undertaken by SDWCLP, the Aga Khan Trust for Culture, and the World Bank teams. The work included (a) a topographic survey of the entirety of WCL to serve as the geographic information system spatial base and to be used for the design of infrastructure;

Map 4.2 Footprint of the Sustainable Development of the Walled City of Lahore Project

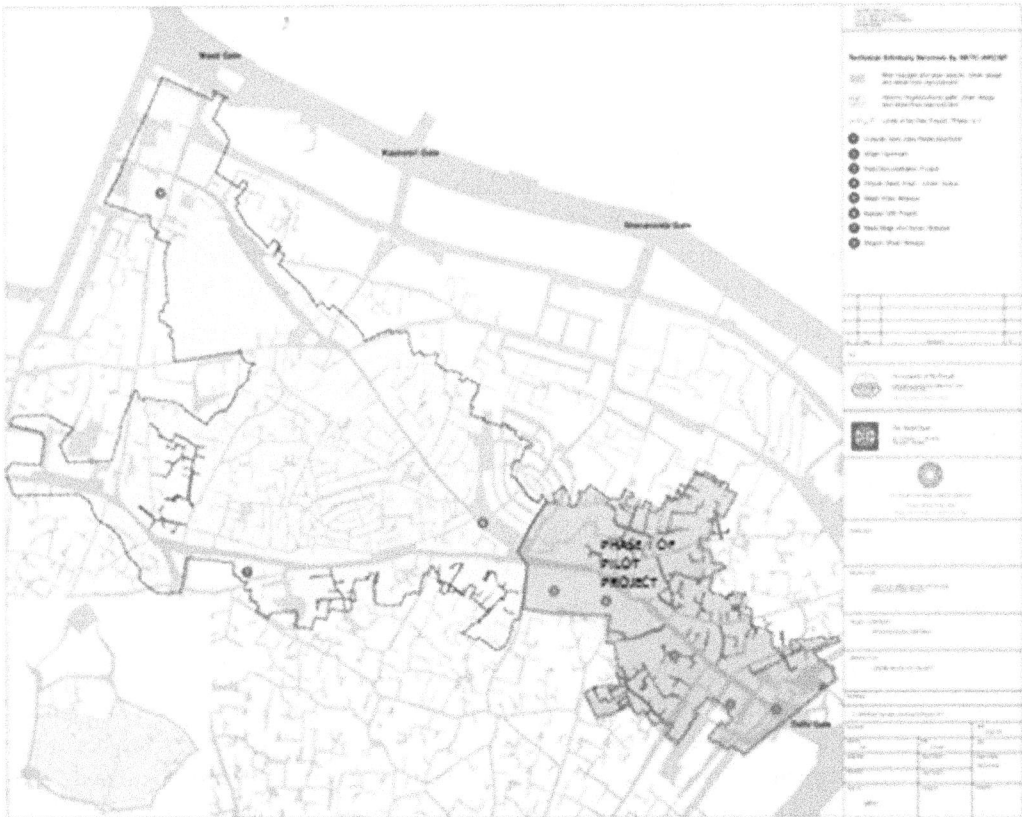

Photo 4.2 Sustainable Development of the Walled City of Lahore Project, Pakistan: Before and After Resettlement

a. Before resettlement   b. After resettlement

(b) an inventory of all historic buildings in WCL, including land-use records, ownership, age, and historic values; (c) a strategic plan for WCL; (d) detailed physical documentation of all buildings in the pilot area; and (e) a socioeconomic household survey across WCL that included 1,757 households.[5] The initiative also included building the capacity of government officials, professionals, and paraprofessionals in specialist skills needed for the preparatory and implementation activities.

The Neighborhood Demonstration Projects

Once the preparatory activities were completed and detailed designs of the infrastructure networks, building facades, and street furniture and paving were developed, the complex nature of the task at hand became even more evident. Such urban regeneration work had never been done before, particularly in such a congested historic environment. Moreover, numerous encroachments on public space had to be removed.

Therefore, a decision was made to test the implementation of the civil works through two neighborhood demonstration projects in Gali Surjan Singh and Muhammadi Muhallah—small, densely populated neighborhoods with main streets emanating from the Royal Trail. The objectives of the two projects were to implement and evaluate design details, methodologies, processes, and techniques to be employed in the pilot project to ensure that they were practical and implementable. Two of the main challenges faced by the neighborhood demonstration projects were to change stakeholder perceptions regarding heritage assets and to sustain community participation in a meaningful manner.

Thematic Analysis
Preparation of Resettlement Action Plan

Because one of the cultural heritage component's objectives was to upgrade capacity of the local government authorities to develop and implement a program to restore and enhance the existing tangible cultural assets, a separate cultural heritage plan was not required. Involuntary resettlement was therefore the principal World Bank safeguard policy triggered by the project. The original project scope included the relocation of shops that were encroaching on the right-of-way and the demolition of extended portions of legal residential constructions within the right-of-way.

The scope of the pilot was soon expanded on technical grounds, because slopes and topography required that networks for water supply, sewage, and drainage could not be restricted to one main street but had to include secondary and tertiary networks. The additional work mainly involved residential neighborhoods along the Royal Trail. Here, the initiative included the removal, relocation, and rebuilding of parts of structures that had encroached onto the streets and public domain.

The RAP was prepared in June 2010. The pilot project originally planned to undertake the removal of 147 shops along the Royal Trail and expected to affect another 732 shops on a temporary basis. An addendum to the RAP was developed and approved in May 2011 to cover the expanded scope of the initiative. It identified 264 kitchens and washrooms constructed as encroachments onto the public realm to be relocated. Key elements of the RAP included public participation and consultation, baseline development of the project area, impact assessment and mitigation, an institutional framework to implement the RAP, mechanisms to address grievances by affected persons during project implementation, and the budget and institutional capacity to implement the RAP. A detailed census preceded the RAP, taking place after information about it had been widely disseminated and an announcement had been made regarding the census cut-off date.

The census listed all properties and occupants in the project area to ensure that new encroachments did not appear after the word had spread about the generous compensation package under the World Bank–funded initiative.

Social Mobilization

SDWCLP had to ensure appropriate skill sets in negotiation and conflict management, and it had to ensure there was a participatory process for social mobilization teams (SMT) for full community participation and implementation of the RAP. To this end, it established an SMT whose objectives were to

- Build awareness by informing, educating, and mobilizing stakeholder communities about the pilot project, its objectives, and its benefits through a series of meetings and consultations.

- Support the formation of female and male community-based organizations (CBOs) and activist groups to develop ownership and communication channels.
- Network with all stakeholders, including civil society organizations, NGOs, government officials, informal shopkeepers, and encroachers working or living in the pilot project area.
- Share details of the plans and the direct impacts on the communities.
- Develop a grievance redress mechanism.
- Train and mentor community youth through a skills enhancement program linked to income-generating opportunities.

The SMT was hired by SDWCLP before the RAP had been formulated. Therefore, it was able to assist in information gathering required for developing the RAP. In the process, the team acquired invaluable on-the-job training and got to know the communities well, advantages that helped begin the process of building lasting relationships between the SMT and community members. Once the RAP was approved, the implementation work was initiated through preliminary consultative meetings.

The SMT conducted more than 1,000 meetings to create awareness among the potential beneficiaries and affected persons of the pilot, including local trade associations. The SMT also identified and trained youth in negotiation and conflict management skills to become activists of a lane or neighborhood in the project area, allowing them to become a part of social activist groups.

Social activist groups were established to coordinate with affected households and to help implement the rehabilitation and resettlement process. They interfaced between SDWCLP and CBOs. They assisted in the negotiation process with property owners on the infrastructure and facade designs; shared details about the extent of needed encroachment removal; signed agreements with property owners about their and SDWCLP's roles and responsibilities; prepared activity schedules and timelines for the removal of encroachments and the implementation of civil works; informed residents before work began on their streets; and provided avenues for conflict resolution through the SMT and the grievance redress committee.

The Grievance Redress Mechanism

The grievance redress mechanism developed under the RAP had two levels of redress. In the first level, the CBOs, social activist groups, and the SMT received all written and verbal complaints, which were recorded and documented by the SMT. If the case was not resolved within 10 days, the case was referred to the Grievance Redressal Committee (GRC)—the second level of redress.

The GRC was composed of the director general of the SDWCLP as the GRC chairperson, the director of infrastructure of the SDWCLP, the district revenue officer, and representatives of affected groups[6] and trade organizations. The GRC process entailed the following:

- Affected persons submit their application to the SDWCLP.
- SDWCLP reviews the case and addresses the issue as per provisions of the RAP in 15 days.

- If resolution is not reached, the case is referred to the GRC.
- If a response is not received from the project within 15 days of receipt, the complainant can send a reminder to the SDWCLP with 15 days' notice to take legal action. Affected persons are exempted from legal fees.

Compensation

Some of the main concerns discussed during the stakeholder meetings were related to the need to sustain livelihoods. The majority—64 percent—of the informal shopkeepers and encroachers were provided with cash compensation. Other PAPs requested the following:

- Shops inside the WCL with the same market value or an alternate space in the Shah Alami Market or the Pakistan Cloth Market, which were major regional markets
- Shops in the Jinnah Market, a property privately owned by a widow that was in close vicinity of the Royal Trail project area
- A formula to be developed for a compensation package.

The SMT and social activist groups first engaged with the encroachers of the Shahi Haman—the 380-year-old Royal Bath just inside the Delhi Gate—where project implementation was to commence. After sustained efforts and difficult negotiations, they succeeded in getting encroachers to agree to relocate outside the WCL, following payment of a mutually negotiated compensation package. In keeping with the requirements of OP 4.12, an entitlement matrix was developed as a part of the RAP, keeping in mind the nature of losses, entitlements, and implementation issues (see table 4.1). This development set a precedent for subsequent negotiations with other encroachers.

In the residential streets, a key issue was that bathrooms and kitchens had been constructed on encroached land at street level, or on balconies protruding onto public space on upper levels. Their removal meant that alternative spaces for

Table 4.1 Entitlement Matrix

Nature of loss	Definition of entitled person	Entitlements	Implementation issues
Loss of shop/ residence by informal settler/ encroacher or unauthorized occupant	Head of household illegally occupying shop/residential land or squatting on the proposed right-of-way as identified by the census survey or as per documentary evidence of payment receipts issued by the owner of the property	• Compensation for the lost structure per the assessed value or price by the revenue department provided it was certified by the landowners per World Bank OP 4.12 • Owner's income below the poverty line • Cash grant for shifting (Rs 10,000) of the shop/house from the defined right-of-way preferences in employment during construction activities as income restoration and rehabilitation measure.	• Cash compensation for structure if recognized by the Department of Revenue • Verification of the owner • Compensation for loss of structure • Transfer or shifting charges as per affected person

Source: World Bank 2010, 2011.

these critical household needs had to be found and the facilities replaced before the encroachments could be removed. This issue had not been anticipated, resulting in additional effort and costs. The technical teams proceeded to carve out spaces for these facilities in the tiny houses, while the SMT sought to convince the households to agree to relocate their bathrooms and kitchens. Because the majority of households could not afford to pay for the costs involved in such an endeavor, it was agreed that they would contribute 5 percent of the cost and the project would fund the rest. During the course of implementation, contributions from households were raised to 15 percent as the beneficiaries realized the benefits of these interventions.

The social mobilization efforts resulted in a number of multisectoral and sustainable development outcomes. Ten CBOs were formed and supported in the project area—many headed by community elders who were highly respected and listened to by others. Technical training was provided to 48 youth in partnership with the Technical Education and Vocational Training Authority,[7] after which many youth found sustainable employment. The Aga Khan Foundation and the SAVIORS Foundation—an NGO working in the health field—established medical camps for hepatitis B and C and also distributed plants for gardening. The responsible local governments coordinated with the SMT for remedial activities to prevent the spread of dengue fever.

Security of Land Tenure and Property Ownership

In the context of resettlement in the WCL, properties encroaching on the public rights-of-way were owned by private individuals and families, the Lahore Municipal Corporation, the State Auqaf Department, the State Archaeology Department, or the Evacuee Trust Property Board. Two types of land-based assets were involved: commercial and residential/commercial structures. No land acquisition was involved, but approximately 147 shops and 264 encroachments on these assets needed removal.

Before the enactment of the Walled City of Lahore Act 2012 and the establishment of the Walled City of Lahore Authority (WCLA), the compensation of land-based assets on cultural heritage sites raised a number of challenges. Although establishment of ownership claims was challenging, it was undertaken to ensure that those affected were eligible for compensation payments either as owners or encroachers. In the end, shop occupancy and ownership were established by census survey or through documentary evidence of receipts of payments issued by the owner agencies of the properties (such as the Auqaf Department, for example).

For compensation, SDWCLP followed the Land Acquisition Act of 1894 (LAA) and the entitlement matrix developed for PAPs in compliance with OP 4.12. The law governs acquisition of land for government development projects, sets the procedures for acquiring private land for projects, and mandates the payment of compensation. It allows for a preliminary survey, provides for the declaration of intended acquisition, deals with detailed surveys and plans, provides for inquiry by the land collector into claims and values, and allows for grievance redress at the district level civil court. The law also sets the compensation levels on the basis of market values. The entitlement matrix allowed for the following:

- Loss of structure—land-based structures were replaced regardless of ownership title to the land.
- Loss of a shop by informal settlers or encroachers—preference was given for employment in construction as income restoration, and cash compensation included shifting the shop and compensation for the lost structure.
- Loss of access to infrastructure services—for example, access to water supply, gas, electricity, sewerage, and telephone was lost, and compensation included restoration of the infrastructure facilities at the project's expense.
- Community facility and common property resources of affected persons were replaced with the same or better quality at project cost.

With the passing of the Walled City of Lahore Act 2012, WCLA has the mandate to register properties and their owners and to maintain a record of owners and occupants of immovable property located within the WCL. The WCLA is also responsible for developing land use plans and building control regulations for the WCL and for approving change of land use requests as well as new constructions.

Gender Inclusion Approaches
Gender was mainstreamed in the RAP; women were included in the surveys, focus group discussions, and group trainings. This inclusion was particularly important because access to, affordability of, and use of infrastructure facilities by women and men were linked to inequalities in intrahousehold relations, property rights, and cultural restrictions. In WCL, the gender ratio was 53 percent male and 47 percent female. For livelihood improvement, the SMT worked to build trade skills in plumbing, masonry, electrification, and carpentry, and developed a partnership with the Technical Education and Vocational Training Authority to provide training programs for local residents.

A gender survey was conducted by female members of the SMT for affected females in the project area. Twenty women were randomly selected as respondents from nine side streets along the Royal Trail. All survey participants wanted better business opportunities; they identified training and capacity building in stitching, teaching, using computers, and cooking as their priority needs. The Technical Education and Vocational Training Authority skills development program trained some of the participants in total station use for the detailed survey of the whole walled city, and the participants were subsequently hired by SDWCLP and the Aga Khan Trust for Culture.[8]

Monitoring and Evaluation
In view of the special nature of the project, monitoring and evaluation were undertaken not so much through a formal system, but more through multiple and frequent missions by the World Bank team to the project area, ensuring that the needs and complaints of the community were heard and addressed.

SDWCLP established a field office in the project area where the SMT and technical supervision staff was based, ensuring that SMT members remained engaged with the community on a full-time basis and that they responded to issues in real time. If problems persisted, they surfaced during the visits by the World Bank task team during its numerous site visits. Frequently, these were coordination issues between the SMT and the technical teams.

Because the SMT and engineers would generally accompany the World Bank task team, issues were immediately discussed. If management attention was needed, the issues were promptly raised with SDWCLP's director general. This approach complemented regular social mobilization implementation activities in which the SMT and project engineers worked side by side to take corrective actions. Monitoring and evaluation activities conducted for the RAP were therefore more informal than would normally be required by policy. However, the RAP was implemented meticulously and thoroughly.

Local Capacity Building for Resettlement

As noted earlier, the scale of encroachment on the public space in the WCL was significant and represented the greatest challenge to the implementation of the pilot project. A large-scale social mobilization effort was undertaken to ensure a careful community-centered implementation of the RAP. Local institutional capacity to implement the RAP was strengthened by training officials of local authorities and members of community organizations in public participation, social mobilization, grievance redress mechanisms, and impact assessment and mitigation.

SDWCLP provided training to the SMT to assist in information gathering for the development of the RAP. Team members were trained in field survey tools including data collection, data entry, and data analysis. Socioeconomic and project information from the surveys were used to determine the potential project impacts and mitigation measures. The SMT was subsequently trained in social mobilization, conflict management, and negotiation to ensure ownership of the resettlement process and to determine compensation through participatory processes. In turn, the SMT provided training in conflict management and negotiation to social activist groups composed of youth from the project lanes and neighborhoods so they could support the implementation of the resettlement process.

Capacity building was also provided to CBOs, the district revenue officers, trade associations, and representatives of affected groups to facilitate implementation of the grievance redress mechanism developed under the RAP. In addition, the SMT developed skills in adaptive management by visiting the project site with World Bank staff and taking corrective actions in areas needing attention.

Local government capacity was strengthened through the environmental and social management framework and the resettlement policy framework prepared for the project. Procedures for consultations with stakeholders, including vulnerable groups, were institutionalized in project activities (World Bank 2014).

Results and Outcomes

Continuous stakeholder engagement around contentious issues led to the identification of innovative solutions and effective implementation of the RAP. SDWCLP has left in place a living model of citizen engagement in heritage restoration, which can serve as a platform for citizen-led regeneration and tourism in the area (photos 4.2a and 4.2b). In undertaking the RAP for the SDWCLP pilot project in the WCL,

> the SDWCL unit was able to successfully pilot resettlement planning and benefit sharing initiatives in a complex urban environment. Some 147 shops and 264 encroachments were removed, and 732 shops were provided temporary support. The scale of consultations was significant, with more than a thousand meetings conducted during RAP implementation. Through creating a replicable model of resettlement and citizen engagement in urban cultural heritage conservation, the project created a demonstration effect and built staff capacity to manage social issues in a complex setting. (World Bank 2014)

"Social mobilization has been the key," said Ahmad Bentarik, a sociologist running the WCLA's effort to win the consent of the local community for the project.[9] "The aim is not to create a museum. Here we have to tackle all issues" (Burke 2013).

The results of the social mobilization process put into place for the pilot project included the following:

- Improved municipal services
- Restored building facades and improved urban streetscape
- Historic dwellings conserved and upgraded with modern facilities
- Increased owner equity participation in successive years—5 percent in 2010; 15 percent in 2011
- Community representatives involved in the maintenance and upkeep of the street
- Youth engaged in all aspects of voluntary work
- Youth willing to pursue or continue higher education
- An increased sense of civic responsibility—for example, no informal connections for power supply for illumination during festivals.

Conclusions

SDWCLP undertook a systematic analysis of urban livelihoods in the project area (MacMahon 2013). Social mobilization processes ensured that urban livelihood reconstruction was informed by baseline studies and by detailed meetings with PAPs, which led to an understanding of their needs and motivations. Most urban involuntary resettlement projects do not give adequate consideration to livelihood issues—a critical aspect in the lives of the urban poor. In fact, a relative neglect of livelihood issues has long been noted as one of the most serious shortfalls of urban resettlement policy (Choi 2013).

An understanding of livelihood concerns was as critical as that of physical assets like housing and shops that were to be restored. The livelihood lens contributed to the fine-tuning of policy responses and reconstruction attempts in a way that was more relevant to urban involuntary resettlement. For the urban poor, the most acute issue can be the loss of physical assets—such as an investment in a structure over time—as well as their productive functioning at the sites of their livelihoods, the true value of which is usually neglected. The main innovative practices and lessons learned from the case study are summarized in boxes 4.4 and 4.5.

Box 4.4 Summary of Innovative Practices

The main innovative practices highlighted in this case study include the following:

- The emphasis put on systematic analysis of urban livelihoods in the project area
- The extent of the social mobilization process put into place to support urban livelihood reconstruction during resettlement implementation
- The efforts engaged in integrating gender perspectives in resettlement design and implementation, including gender surveys and targeted training activities for women
- The strengthening of local institutional capacity to implement the resettlement action plan through training of local authorities and community associations in impact assessment and mitigation, grievance redress mechanisms, public participation, and social mobilization.

Box 4.5 Key Lessons Learned

- A multisectoral approach is important.
- A paradigm shift is required in the perception of cultural heritage assets.
- Heritage conservation needs to focus on both tangible and intangible heritage assets.
- Insights into socioeconomic aspects are critical to success.
- Heritage-related initiatives require patience and perseverance.
- Good social mobilization pays huge dividends.
- A livelihoods lens beyond mere land acquisition is necessary.
- Important interdependencies exist between a historic core and the surrounding metropolitan area.
- Public sector officials can feel challenged by new ideas.
- Multiple interactions and site visits for learning on the job provide invaluable insights into the needs and priorities of beneficiaries and affected persons.
- Piloting and testing processes in complex settings before scaling up can pay huge dividends.
- Success depends greatly on institutional capacity in requisite fields.
- Cultural heritage asset restoration can contribute to mitigating poverty and enhancing shared prosperity.

Source: Arshad 2012.

Notes

1. Medina is the old Arab or non-European quarter of a North African town.
2. The architectural design concept for the reconfigured PLY was agreed to on the basis of an international competition funded by the Millennium Challenge Corporation in 2009–10.
3. A year after the end of the compact, delays were still being experienced by subcontractors in acquiring titles to their units from the government of Morocco and in being provided with technical assistance to manage the building as a collective unit.
4. The initiative was instrumental in attracting the interest of the Aga Khan Trust for Culture in mid-2008. The trust signed a private-public partnership agreement with GoPunjab. It provided technical assistance for preparatory activities with requisite experts on topics that included heritage restoration and strategic planning for historic areas.
5. The sample represented 8 percent of the estimated population.
6. Affected groups include resident owners who live in the area and have their own shop; nonresident owners who live outside the Walled City and have their own property on the Royal Trail; resident tenants who run their shops, pay rent, and reside within the walled city; nonresident tenants who run their shop but do not reside inside the Walled City; and encroachers and informal occupants.
7. The Technical Education and Vocational Training Authority was formed through an ordinance by the governor of Punjab to enhance the global competitiveness of Punjab with a quality and productive workforce by developing a demand-driven, standardized, dynamic, and integrated technical education and vocational training service.
8. A total station is an electronic/optical instrument used in modern surveying and building construction.
9. In the later years of the project, SDWCLP was transformed into the Walled City of Lahore Authority, established under the Walled City of Lahore Act of 2012 and developed with the project's assistance.

References

Arshad, Shahnaz. 2012. "Creating the Enabling Environment in the Walled City of Lahore: Supporting Historic Cities, Cultural Heritage, and Sustainable Tourism." Lecture presented at the Urban Forum. http://siteresources.worldbank.org/INTURBAN DEVELOPMENT/Resources/336387-1330357378410/8468721-1331160207484 /Arshad.pdf.

Burke, Jason. 2013. "Lahore Authorities Battle to Restore Splendour of Ancient Wall." *Guardian*, May 26. http://www.theguardian.com/world/2013/may/26/lahore-walled -city-pakistan.

Choi, Narae. 2013. "Idea Note for Urban Involuntary Resettlement." World Bank, Washington, DC.

Ebbe, Katrinka. 1998. "Conservation in the Old Walled City of Lahore." *Cultural Heritage: Landmarks of a New Generation. Urban Age Special Issue* (September): 14.

MacMahon, Philippa. 2013. "Nothing Left to Lose: The Role of Labour Market Experiences in Development-Induced Displacement and Resettlement." Paper of the International Conference on Development-Induced Displacement and Resettlement, Oxford, U.K., March.

World Bank. 2006. PSMIP Project Appraisal Document. Report No. 32156-PK, Energy and Infrastructure Unit, South Asia Region, May 8, World Bank, Washington, DC.

———. 2010. "Sustainable Development of the Walled City of Lahore Project." Resettlement Action Plan, Draft Report. Prepared by M. Aslam Malik, World Bank, Pakistan.

———. 2011. "Sustainable Development of the Walled City of Lahore Project." Resettlement Action Plan. Addendum to Resettlement Action Plan for the Streets Adjacent to the Royal Trail, World Bank, Pakistan.

———. 2014. "Punjab Municipal Services Improvement Project." Implementation Completion and Results Report 3023, World Bank, Washington, DC. http://documents .worldbank.org/curated/en/139061468284108408/pdf/ICR30230P083920IC0 disclosed06040140.pdf.

———. n.d. "From Concept to Reality: Lessons Learned from Designing and Preparing the Fez, Morocco Cultural Heritage Project." Annex 3, World Bank, Washington, DC.

Suggested Reading

Unité de Gestion de Projet (UGP)/Agence de Dédensification et de Réhabilitation de Fès (ADER-Fès). 2011. "Projet Artisanat et Fès Médina. Agence pour le Partenariat et le Progrès (APP) et Millennium Challenge Corporation (MCC)." Plan d'Action de Réinstallation—Rapport final, préparé par A. Bouziane, Prof. de Sociologie, Université de Fès, avec l'appui de G. Appleby, UGP/ADER-Fès.

CHAPTER 5

Conclusions and Recommendations

Addressing the Challenges of Urban Resettlement

The urbanization trend of the past 50 years will surely continue; an estimated 2.7 billion people will move to cities by 2030 (Joshi-Ghani 2013). Areas experiencing slower urbanization will probably catch up with more urban cities, and a significant part of the new or expanding urban areas will be in Asia and Africa. Urbanization and the need for complex land acquisition and involuntary resettlement will follow hand in hand. The challenges of managing dense urban areas, with the accompanying need for transportation, water management, and social services, will be significant.

It is difficult to separate the strict resettlement of project-affected people from programs and policies benefiting urban spaces and social services in contemporary urban areas. Resettlement is often intertwined with housing programs, blurring the boundaries between affected people and beneficiaries. Urban planning and the displacement of poor urban populations to city outskirts through gentrification processes also raise important issues related to social exclusion and marginalization.

Because of the density of areas to be resettled, urban resettlement often involves challenges of scale. The large number of people to be resettled, the financial and human resources needed, and the difficulties involved in managing projects of such magnitude make resettlements complex endeavors. Nevertheless, urban resettlements differ from rural resettlements in a number of ways beyond the issues of magnitude and spatial density. Urban settlements densely occupy space in a way that is characterized by specific social networks and complex economic relationships. Often, informality of tenure and economic activities figures prominently as a concern, adding additional challenges to resettlement implementation.

Some of the issues specific to urban resettlement have to do with the rural-urban transition itself. This is true both in terms of the transition of rural populations to urban areas and economic activities and in terms of the transformation of rural and periurban spaces into urban ones. Evaluation, compensation, and replacement value take on new levels of complexity. Similarly, because of the density of urban areas and the resulting characteristics of urban transportation networks, land situated in adequate locations for resettlement destination areas is scarce.

Delays, budget overruns, and other unexpected occurrences with urban resettlement projects are compounded by challenges of scale. Everything that is challenging in the resettlement process, including enumerating the affected population, defining eligibility for compensation and assistance, and managing civil works, becomes more difficult when the numbers affected are large and when economic activities and land occupation are informal. Unforeseen circumstances commonly create difficulties. Because of this uncertainty, significant variations in initial projected resettlement budgets for a single project should be considered good practice when integrated into overall project planning.

This report covered several aspects of urban involuntary resettlement in each case study. However, the cases in the report focused on three main issues or areas of innovation in urban involuntary resettlement: innovative country systems, relocation of informal urban settlements, and livelihood restoration for informal urban occupations. The following three sections summarize the main conclusions drawn from the case studies for each of these issues. The final section summarizes the findings and recommendations of the report.

Innovative Country Systems

Resettlement is a development issue that goes beyond safeguard policies. There is a growing recognition that urban issues reach beyond questions of policy management. This understanding is clearly indicated by the use of housing programs as a solution to resettling populations with the inclusion of infrastructure development, disaster risk management, and the tackling of existing gaps in housing solutions for low-income citizens, as illustrated in the Brazilian case study included in this report.

Globally, there is progress in the adoption of legal frameworks that are aligned with international resettlement standards, such as in the cases of Brazil and India. However, a great deal remains to be achieved in most countries to change approaches that rely mainly on compensation toward more comprehensive processes capable of ensuring the restoration of living conditions and livelihoods for resettled populations.

Some of the benefits of adopting good practices at the national level are as follows:

- Obvious benefits with regard to social development and poverty alleviation
- Mitigation of risks to reputation
- Mitigation of social risks and avoidance of conflicts linked to land acquisition and resettlement

- Minimization of risks of project delays and cost overruns
- Facilitated access to international public and private financing because resettlement has become a requirement of most international financing institutions and large commercial bank signatories of the Equator Principles.

It is clear that, as a notion, resettlement presents limitations to understanding the complex phenomenon of causes, solutions, and policies connected to urban displacement. Displacement caused by diffuse changes like gentrification—or even displacement that is triggered by infrastructure projects—is clearly connected to public policies, housing gaps in urban areas, and social services. The problem of displacement by development projects and resettlement of project-displaced people exists in contexts of urban spatial and social services planning and implementation. Multidimensional problems cannot be solved with one-dimensional solutions. Whereas safeguard policies play an important role in resettlements—and always will—they need to be applied in tandem with large-scale policy approaches. The development of country systems is part of the wider view on how to address problems relating to resettlements. A good example of this is presented in the case study on the 2013 Brazilian ordinance on involuntary resettlement that seamlessly connects with the Brazilian federal housing program with its complementary approach to the provision of social services.

What does it mean to support the development of country systems for social and environmental management? Following the successful example of the cooperation between the World Bank and the Ministry of Cities of Brazil, it means developing organic relationships. It means helping to create innovative solutions for a country's problems. It requires persistence throughout the length of the process, allowing time for the development of relationships, the engagement of stakeholders, and maturing of the dialogue. Beyond those requirements, there remains the challenge of helping build capacity for resettlement in the context of the relative regulatory and administrative autonomy of a large number of municipalities, each with its own issues and capacity challenges. The significant results that can be achieved at a very low cost through such capacity building processes justify the effort.

Relocation of Informal Urban Settlements

Both case studies reviewed under this theme reveal the importance of participative resettlement censuses and surveys in large informal settlements and World Bank efforts to support capacity building for relocation of informal urban settlements.

The highly challenging Mumbai Urban Transportation Project (MUTP) in India was remarkable for its use of participatory slum enumeration and resettlement planning with the assistance of local nongovernmental organizations. This was also the case for the Urban Development Project in Nouakchott, Mauritania, which was particularly noteworthy for its development of an integrated urban planning approach in which resettlement operations conducted for displaced households in the El Mina slum dovetailed with urban renewal operations for the majority of households remaining in the slum.

The MUTP supported the development of a guidance note on urban resettlement (World Bank and Government of Maharashtra 2009) that was prepared on the basis of workshops with representatives from other Indian cities involved in urban slum clearance programs (Chennai, Delhi, and Hyderabad). The Urban Development Project sponsored the development of a specialized El Mina sourcebook (World Bank 2007) on urban slum rehabilitation and clearance programs that was subsequently used by the government of Mauritania for similar operations conducted in other slums of the capital city and other regional cities without donor support. These capacity-building initiatives are creditworthy and have contributed to the development of better country systems for involuntary resettlement.

Livelihood Restoration for Informal Urban Occupations

The two case studies reviewed under this theme demonstrate the importance of quality socioeconomic baseline surveys for (a) identifying livelihood restoration needs related to informal urban occupations, (b) the critical role played by social mobilization and grievance mechanisms in the management of complex operations involving the restoration of informal sector livelihoods in urban environments, and (c) the need for adapted monitoring and evaluation processes to assess the outcomes of livelihood restoration measures and to make adjustments as needed.

Both the Artisan and Fez Medina Project, funded by the Millennium Challenge Corporation in Morocco, and the Sustainable Development of Walled City in Lahore Project in Pakistan, funded by the World Bank, undertook systematic analyses of urban livelihoods in the project areas. Social mobilization processes ensured that there was a grasp of urban livelihood reconstruction through baseline studies and through detailed meetings with project-affected persons that led to an understanding of their needs and motivations—a critical aspect of the life of the urban poor that does not receive the consideration and attention it deserves in the planning of urban involuntary resettlement projects. This relative neglect of livelihood issues has, in fact, been noted as one of the most serious shortfalls of urban resettlement for some time.

The combination of continuous stakeholder engagement and adaptive management led to agreement on contentious issues, innovative solutions, and effective implementation of the resettlement action plans. Both projects highlight the important requirements of complex urban resettlement activities in relation to the supervision and oversight resources that must be deployed by funding agencies throughout the planning and implementation process.

Both projects also offer fascinating perspectives on resettlement operations conducted in heritage urban centers. They have each left in place living models of citizen engagement in heritage restoration, which can serve as platforms for citizen-led regeneration and tourism.

Main Findings and Recommendations

Although the challenges of each urban resettlement project are somewhat unique, there are commonalities among successful approaches, some of which have been promoted by resettlement specialists for a long time. These factors of success are summarized as follows:

- *Transparency and participation.* Sometimes seen by resettlement implementers as weakening their negotiating position, transparency and participation actually increase the likelihood of successful outcomes. The Mumbai case study was remarkable for its use of participatory slum enumeration and resettlement planning with the assistance of local nongovernmental organizations. The Lahore case study featured a highly successful model of social mobilization for attaining buy-in and engagement from project-affected persons.

- *Understanding of informal economic and social networks.* All four of the project-specific case studies in this report highlight the need to properly understand informal economic and social networks affected by resettlement and to define areas of influence and impacts of resettlement operations. This is largely done through participatory studies carried out in informal residential and commercial communities, including through systematic analysis of informal urban livelihoods—as illustrated in the Fez and Lahore case studies—or through self-administered surveys with local nongovernmental organizations—as illustrated in the Mumbai case study.

- *Adaptive management of resettlement operations.* Backed by contingency budgeting and integrated activity scheduling, adaptive management of resettlement operations can help address unforeseen challenges related to the high level of complexity of urban areas and their related economic and social networks. Equally important are additional supervision resources during resettlement implementation. The need for thorough planning is central, but a resettlement plan cannot be expected to cover all outcomes at this level of complexity. Successful urban resettlement projects are generally supported by flexible and adaptive planning and implementation processes and by appropriate financial resources.

- *Post-resettlement socioeconomic surveys and independent monitoring and evaluation.* Although resettlement monitoring activities were regularly conducted for all four of the project-specific case studies covered in this report throughout resettlement implementation, large-scale socioeconomic surveys to evaluate the extent to which resettlement outcomes were successful and livelihoods were restored after project completion was done for only one of the case study projects—the Mauritania Urban Development Project. These surveys were complemented by independent monitoring and evaluation. Such good practices should be encouraged and budgets provided for them in complex urban resettlement operations.

- *Local capacity building and dissemination of good urban resettlement practices.* The case studies highlighted the importance of local capacity building in ensuring successful outcomes in urban resettlement. Training, public awareness, and specialized technical assistance funded through the Artisan and Fez Medina Project enabled municipal agencies and concerned populations (1) to gain a better understanding of resettlement processes conducted according to international standards and (2) to compare the results obtained with previously unsuccessful resettlement efforts conducted in compliance with national standards. In Lahore, institutional capacity to implement the resettlement action plan was strengthened through training local authorities and community associations in impact assessment and mitigation, grievance redress mechanisms, public participation, and social mobilization. The development of specialized resettlement sourcebooks for informal urban settlements in the Mumbai and Nouakchott projects also contributed to the dissemination of best practices in other Indian and Mauritanian cities.

- *Integrating the planning of urban resettlement into a wider municipal urban planning and housing policy context.* As illustrated by the Mumbai and Nouakchott case studies, the success of urban resettlement programs is largely linked to their successful integration into the wider context of urban development and renewal. This successful integration was illustrated in the Mumbai case study when the Maharashtra state government encouraged private sector participation in the resettlement program by offering additional development rights or transfer of development rights and floor space index to private developers willing to resettle slum dwellers in modern buildings at their own cost. This was also illustrated in the Nouakchott case study, which was particularly noteworthy for its development of an integrated urban planning approach in which resettlement operations conducted for displaced households in the El Mina slum dovetailed with urban renewal operations for the majority of households remaining in the slum.

- *Strengthening of country systems.* Whereas most countries have well-enshrined eminent domain and expropriation laws and procedures, only a limited number of countries have legal frameworks and procedures aimed at ensuring that land acquisition and involuntary resettlement go beyond compensation for lost assets and requiring that affected livelihoods be restored or even improved. Efforts at strengthening country systems aim to address those gaps. Although the application of international resettlement standards continues to be of central importance in development projects, initiatives to strengthen country systems for urban resettlement and urban planning also allow for a more systemic approach at the national level, building capacity and integrating involuntary resettlement and land acquisition into the larger context of urban development and housing policies and programs.

Clearly, there is a need to further establish links between urban planning and housing policies on the one hand and urban involuntary resettlement practices on the other. These links could involve, for instance, promoting innovative in situ approaches to urban resettlement. Urban involuntary resettlement requirements could combine curative measures—such as upgrading slums to address existing substandard housing stock, lack of security of tenure, and poor public infrastructure and services—with preventive measures, such as providing affordable land and housing development through formal channels to address the flow of new housing demands. This report has not touched on important issues related to the functioning of urban land markets and housing market dynamics in cities and historic centers or their links to urban involuntary resettlement. A dedicated urban and social working group should be set up by the World Bank to further explore these issues.

References

Joshi-Ghani, Abha. 2013. "Rethinking Cities." *People, Spaces, Deliberation* (blog), World Bank, October 28. http://blogs.worldbank.org/publicsphere.

World Bank. 2007. "L'opération de réinstallation des ménages déplacés par la restructuration du quartier précaire d'El Mina à Nouakchott—Sourcebook—Opération 2000–2007." El-Mina Resettlement Operation Sourcebook, produced for the Urban Development Project Task Team, World Bank, Washington, DC.

World Bank and Government of Maharashtra. 2009. *India—Mumbai Urban Transport Project: Guidance Note on Urban Resettlement.* Washington, DC: World Bank.

Environmental Benefits Statement

The World Bank Group is committed to reducing its environmental footprint. In support of this commitment, we leverage electronic publishing options and print-on-demand technology, which is located in regional hubs worldwide. Together, these initiatives enable print runs to be lowered and shipping distances decreased, resulting in reduced paper consumption, chemical use, greenhouse gas emissions, and waste.

We follow the recommended standards for paper use set by the Green Press Initiative. The majority of our books are printed on Forest Stewardship Council (FSC)–certified paper, with nearly all containing 50–100 percent recycled content. The recycled fiber in our book paper is either unbleached or bleached using totally chlorine-free (TCF), processed chlorine–free (PCF), or enhanced elemental chlorine–free (EECF) processes.

More information about the Bank's environmental philosophy can be found at http://www.worldbank.org/corporateresponsibility.

green press INITIATIVE

www.ingramcontent.com/pod-product-compliance
Lightning Source LLC
Chambersburg PA
CBHW080426270326
41929CB00018B/3183